HONOUR SATISFIED

HONOUR SATISFIED

A Dorset Rifleman
at War
1916–1918
2nd Lieutenant
Frank Warren

Edited by Antony Bird

The Crowood Press

First published in 1990 by
The Crowood Press
Gipsy Lane, Swindon,
Wiltshire SN2 6DQ

British Library Cataloguing in Publication Data
Warren, Frank
  Honour satisfied: a Dorset rifleman at war, 1916–18.
  1. World War 1. Army operations by Great Britain. Army –
Biographies
  I. Title II. Bird, Antony
  940.48141

ISBN 1–85223–540–3

All illustrations by courtesy of Royal Green
Jackets Museum, Winchester.

Phototypeset by Input Typesetting Ltd, London
Printed in Great Britain by Billing & Sons Ltd, Worcester

Contents

Acknowledgements   vii
Introduction   1

The War Diary of 2nd Lieutenant F.
Warren, R/22817, 20th Battalion, Kings
Royal Rifle Corps, BEF

1   October 1916 to February 1917:   7
     The Somme
2   September 1917 to January 1918:   49
     The Ypres Salient
3   March 1918: The German Attack   75

Acknowledgements

My thanks are due to Col Ian McCausland (Retd) of the Royal Green Jackets for his kindness in making the diary available for publication. Thanks are also due to Ivor Snook and Jim Moriarty of the Royal Green Jackets Museum for their assistance in providing photographs and answering enquiries.

A. E. A. B.
1989

Introduction

The bare facts of Frank Warren's war are easily spelt out. On 25th October 1916 he arrived in France aged nineteen years, with a wife and two children at home in Dorset. Although he was a sergeant in the 3rd Battalion, the Dorset Regiment, he was posted on arrival to the 20th (New Army) Battalion of the Kings Royal Rifle Corps (60th Rifles) which was serving as a pioneer battalion, attached to the 3rd Division – although interestingly enough Warren never mentions the division to which he is attached. He stayed with the KRRC until the end of his war in 1918, transferring to the 17th Battalion as a 2nd Lieutenant on his second tour of duty starting in October 1917. It was not unusual for drafts of soldiers to be posted to whatever formations had available vacancies at the time. The regiment, ranking 60th in the line, was raised in 1755 to fight in North America; it was then known as the 60th Royal Americans and was composed mainly of foreign, and chiefly German, mercenaries.

He was granted compassionate leave at the end of this second tour of duty on the death of his father in January 1918 and returned to France less than two months later to be plunged into the retreat following the great German offensive which started on 21st March 1918. During the first ten days of the retreat he clearly showed his abilities as an outstanding young officer. The diary ends with him being wounded in the back of the head and evacuated to a hospital in Rouen.

Both the 20th and the 17th Battalions KRRC were formed in 1915 as service or new army battalions by the British Empire League in London, and subsequently taken over by the War Office. Altogether the KRRC raised 23 new battalions during the course of the war, in addition to the six regular battalions based in Winchester. Rifle battalions, by the time of the First World War, used the same weapons and equipment as other infantry battalions and had ceased to perform their original role as specialist riflemen. The 20th Pioneer Battalion performed trench work, wiring and carrying, although of course all frontline troops were required to carry out these tasks. As a pioneer it was, however, less likely to be ordered into attack. The 17th Battalion was reorganised in April 1918 and became the 2nd Composite Battalion. The battalions of the corps were distributed throughout the British Army; in this sense it was not a 'corps' at all in the normal military sense of the term.

A wealth of first-hand material is here set down (illegally) by Warren, written from memory soon after the events described and eventually arriving in the safe-keeping of the KRRC (Green Jackets) Museum in Winchester. A conscientious and intelligent soldier with a keen eye for detail, he was an eager student of all things military. His first tour of duty was spent in the Somme battlefield after the costly and grim infantry fighting had ground to a halt. His second tour, as a 2nd Lieutenant with the 17th Battalion and with a new baby born during his leave, was spent in the Ypres Salient of which he writes, in almost biblical vein: 'It is a wilderness and a solitary place, nothing whole remains.'

Here conditions were perhaps at their worst in the whole war. Sir Philip Gibbs has written (*Realities of War*, Heinemann 1920): 'For the first time the British Army lost its spirit of optimism . . . ' Yet Warren did not lose his spirit. When he is offered the chance of a safer job with the Quartermaster, he turns it down, saying he is 'not keen on that branch of the work'. Once again, though, he is fortunate – if that is the word – in joining the battalion towards the end of that particularly brutish campaign. He is indeed fortunate when an attack in which his battalion was to have taken part is 'put off or given over to other troops', in Warren's uncharacteristically vague words. But the Salient was, of course, an extremely dangerous place to be, whether attacking or not. In one four-day spell in the front line, Warren's half company of 34 men suffered three killed and several wounded. This was, in the grim phrase of the time, 'normal wastage'.

The bombardment which heralded the German offensive of 21st March 1918 was the most intense of the whole war: 6,473 guns opened up before dawn on the 40 mile front of the 5th Army (in which the 17th Battalion was serving) and the southern part of the 3rd Army. Warren's account of his ten days of the German attack, of retreat, near-rout and counter-attack on the old Somme battlefield, is a very valuable historical document. As H. Essame has written (*The Battle for Europe 1918*, Batsford 1972), 'to give even an impression of what actually happened to the Fifth Army, so local was the experience of survivors and so inadequate are the regimental records, is a baffling task'. We know now that, in their attempt to rout the British and French Armies before the Americans could play an effective part in the war, and with reinforcements from the Eastern Front to swell their ranks, the Germans took ground more than 40 miles deep in some places. We know also that before their attack finally petered out the Germans suffered 28,000 killed and 250,000 wounded, and inflicted a total of 240,000 casualties on the British 3rd and 5th Armies, of which Warren was one.

Warren, who could only know what was happening on his front and immediate flanks, has written an account which adds flesh and blood to these grim statistics, an account which must surely rank alongside the great classic *Old Soldiers Never Die* by Frank Richards. During the course of a few days Warren is bombarded by German artillery and field guns, attacked by low-flying aircraft ('uncomfortable') and fired on by machine guns and rifles, as well as by snipers on his own side; and yet even after six days of retreat, 'each man has his rifle and his pouches full of ammunition; he is not dismayed and is perfectly ready to put up a fight when and where he has a sporting chance'. It is this attitude of mind that ultimately helped bring the German attack to a halt.

But this diary is more than just a valuable historical document. It is a work of considerable literary merit. Warren's accounts of the blowing of the bridge on the Somme canal, and the rescue of the guns at Mircourt, are wonderful set piece descriptions which must be among the most graphic of all accounts of events on a battlefield. His descriptions of soldiers dangling their legs from the railway waggons on the way up to the front in 1916, and of bully-beef tins being thrown from hand to hand in the front line in March 1918, are brilliantly evocative images of the war.

The diary is published here almost entirely as originally written by Frank Warren.

Antony Bird
Chichester
1989

THE WAR DIARY OF 2ND LIEUTENANT F WARREN

R/22817, 20th Battalion, Kings Royal Rifle Corps, BEF

1
October 1916 to February 1917: The Somme

[*Tuesday, 24th October 1916*]

[Our] special troop train ran through Winchester about 1 p.m. At Southampton Docks the train ran straight into one of the huge embarkation sheds, covering a space as large as the nave of Winchester Cathedral. Close to one side the train came to a stop, the men disentrained and formed up across the hall. Their time was their own until 3.30 p.m. but no one was allowed to post a letter or pass the dock gates. There was much of interest in the Docks, certain war vessels not to be detailed here, and some interest was shown in the large troopship in which we were to cross the Channel. On this most of the men were employed for a couple [of hours] in shipping a heavy mail.

At last about 6 p.m. the troops went on board, first placing their packs in the hold, then each man donning a lifebelt and being told off to a place in the lifeboats. Soon after 8 p.m. the boat was off and most of the men settled to sleep in the hold.

Imagine a large square boarded room in the bottom of the ship, approached only by means of a wide ladder stairway which also gave means of ventilation. Round the four sides a gallery, wide and strongly built. In this were many stalls filled with horses and mules shipped at Southampton. The scene from half way down the ladder was a strange one. Several hundred men stretched all over the floor trying to snatch some sleep, others smoking quietly, a few circles of men busy with a game of cards; the stamping of horses in the gallery, the curious shrill bray of the hungry mules; muffled sounds of stamping and shouting on deck – and the wonder was that so many slept so soundly.

For myself I chose a sheltered spot on deck and settled down with my lifebelt as a pillow. The boat was a slow one, but well loaded and riding steadily, in spite of a heavy swell with the wind breaking the wave tops into white horses.

On leaving Southampton Water all lights were extinguished, there was no moon and only the circling gleam of searchlights on the destroyer escort broke the darkness. The ship seemed to be steered on an erratic

7

course, moving in long snaky curves.[1] Each time she changed course she pitched and rolled until she settled down to steady progress once more. This was too much for my seamanship, and the rest of the night was not wholly comfortable.

But there were duties to be done. At 3.30 a day's ration had to be drawn for the men – a tin of bully beef, a slice of cheese, a tin of jam among five or six, and four army biscuits apiece. These were shared out in the hold of the ship; the last share-out saw me bolt suddenly to the upper deck! There I sat for some time until growing daylight showed the distant cliffs of France through the morning mist.

[*Wednesday, 25th October*]

Gradually we drew nearer and two black-grey French torpedo boats took up the work of escort to the harbour. Le Havre shows a fine front to the sea, with a background of green hills and distant woods with but a slight tinge of autumn tints – for the season here seems to be several weeks later than in England.

We draw slowly nearer to the harbour and turn even more slowly to tie up at one of the inner berths. German prisoners are at work in the Docks and we pass close to them. Some of them even make a show of grinning derisively and a few of our men are led to howl at them with the evident wish they had them at the bayonet's point!

At last we are safely moored, and men and horses descend a steep gangway to a large shed. Here the men fall out for a short while and a lady in charge of a coffee stall is kept busily employed. Some of the horses are much exhausted by the journey and require treatment to revive them.

We fall in once more and march off six miles to the Base Camp, the men noting their new surroundings with evident pleasure and with the Englishman's curious sense of satisfaction with his own national institutions. There are perhaps five or six hundred of us all told, and there are not a few wavings of hands and words of welcome, while small children with open hand ask for 'one pennie'.

It is but October, yet the roads are a mass of liquid mud. Through this we trudge full of thoughts of the purpose of our visit which was only too plainly revealed by our busy surroundings. German prison camps are numerous and new roads, camps and munition dumps show their handiwork. On we go up the valley, turning almost due north and at length marching into No. 9 Camp, Infantry Base Depot No. 1, pitched on the steep western slopes of the valley.

We are late in arriving, for the boat took 13 hours from port to port

---

[1] i.e. to avoid submarines.

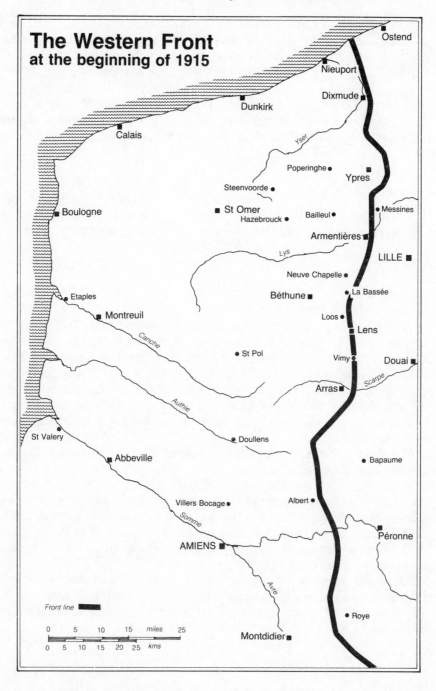

The Western Front at the beginning of 1915

– and the routine of inspections began almost at once. We look out over the valley, and lovely ridges of wooded hills rise before us on the other side. The beautiful crocheted spire of Harfleur cuts the sky line, and the bells ring out in deep rich tones – maybe for the brilliant French success of Verdun.

The rows of tents are pitched fairly far apart, and deep gulleys carry off the surface water from the hills above. Each row boasts of a narrow plank pathway, leading on to the main path below and thence on to the roadway.

[*Thursday, 26th October*]

A wet day and little work to do. Another medical inspection and then Colonel's inspection; and then we are left to our own devices. Cleaning of rifles, letter and diary writing fill the time.

[*Friday, 27th October*]

Reveille at 5.30, parade at 7.15.

Off we march, through liquid mud, up a steep track winding to the hilltops above and behind our camps. Here a huge plateau with more camps spread over its extent, and training grounds stretch far and wide. A huge parade ground with guide-posts for the many regiments assembled. We are given over to an instructor who marches us off to a bayonet fighting course not so very different from the home product. The men are put through their paces whilst sergeants act as assistants to the instructors.

At half past ten comes a break of half an hour. Then more bayonet fighting, this time under an instructor – a Canadian who is a past master at his work, and a wit and satirist to boot. He shows the work of 'the nut', the 16-stone man trained on 'regimental' lines, and his conversion to more forceful ways – so that he carries off the whole of the inside of the sack with the vigour of his reinforced work. Then comes the practical work down a miniature 'Front' – British trench, shell-holes, German lines, 'wood', wire – all found.

Pouring rain brings us home early to spend the time in the comfortable little Sergeants' Mess, with French billiards, or writing or reading.

I have omitted to say I was posted on arrival to the 20th Battalion (Pioneers), KRR.

[*Saturday, 28th October*]

Usual routine of morning parade. Our work consists of instruction in the latest fashions of wire entanglements, and it is full of interest.

French concertina wire and the method of weaving it round ground posts is all new to me. We erect an entanglement section.

[*Sunday, 29th October*]

Pouring rain·most of the morning. A game of solo whist with the Corporals three (Martin, Hodgson and Vickers). Then Church parade was cancelled. Later, strange contrast, made my way to Church Hut in Camp 15 for HC. Wrote and read in my tent most of the afternoon and attended six o'clock service.

[*Monday, 30th October*]

Wet all day, and time devoted to camp 'internal economy'. More letter writing, arranged for washing clothes, and other wants filled.

[*Tuesday, 31st October*]

A fine day on the hill-top – the base training ground. First a lecture on the Mills bomb, followed by 'trench warfare' with dummy bombs, in which I was told off as thrower to the bombing party. Next a lecture by a sniping officer with demonstration of new appliances. After dinner a lecture by Canadian Major with full flavoured Colonial tone – on trench warfare and the laying out of trenches.

[*Wednesday, 1st November*]

Bayonet fighting on the hill all day. Men went down two 'final assault' courses. A new set of German prisoners in camp enclosure seemed much interested in the bayonet practice.

[*Thursday, 2nd November*]

A wet morning. Marched to YMCA Cinema for lectures on 'Bombing' and 'Modern Methods in the Attack'. In afternoon on hill for more bombing practice.

[*Friday, 3rd November*]

Left camp at 6.15 a.m. in charge of fatigue party for work in Havre Dockyard. Took tram near Soldiers' Club and travelled pretty comfortably down to Docks. Tram conductor, a middle-aged, ill looking man, wore the ribbon of the Croix de Guerre and showed a bullet hole through his disabled right wrist, one through both jaws and indicated a third

11

through his right leg. Marched into Docks and was told off with thirty men to help unload a cargo of sandbags, one of several shiploads in from Calcutta. The cranes hoist huge bales from the ship's hold. The iron bands are severed with a hatchet by men of the navvy battalion who place large bundles, each containing 2,000 bags, on to hand barrows. These are wheeled away over the cobblestones to the waiting railway trucks and this work falls to the lot of the soldiers. To keep the men to their work and maintain a constant of trucks is my work.

In following up the trucks through the Docks, one sees something of the huge work of waging a modern war. There are reels and reels of barbed wire, forming small hills of reddy brown hue; huge stacks of millions of sandbags; acres of shovels, fields of Lewis gun carriages and other munitions, all showing the vastness of the scale on which this war is being waged.

Among the ships at the Quay side is the huge black shape of the 'Archimedes', the vessel on which we crossed the Channel. She is fitted mainly as a cargo vessel and carries a heavy load. The harbour has been closed for nearly a week and there was a crowd of vessels to be unloaded.

We carried on with the work until nearly dusk and then returned, 66 in one car, to our camp quarters. One incident of the day was the sight of an officer's kitbag with the lettering 'Lieut. C.W. Breadmore, ASC'.[2] I spoke to the orderly and found that Breadmore had just arrived from leave in England.

[*Saturday, 4th November*]

Up 'the hill' again to the Central Training School and we are told off to-day for gas drill. A large hut half underground and we are drawn up in single file with gas helmets on. All file through a dense atmosphere of poison gas and come slowly out into the fresh air, smelling strongly of chlorine. All metal work was heavily tarnished and we congratulated ourselves on our black bone buttons. Next came a test of tear gas from a grenade exploded in a covered trench.

Half an hour's 'break' and well grown French girls turn many a penny with cakes, apples and chocolate at twopence each item! A procession of black clad folk approaches and proves to be a wedding party. Bridegroom silver haired and jaunty. Bride, who led all the way by half a length, dressed in orthodox veil and swaying strangely as she bumped along on a wooden leg! So they passed along amid encouraging remarks offered in all politeness by 'the boys'.

The afternoon was spent in letter writing, a bath and other camp duties. Heavy rain in night.

[2] Army Service Corps.

12

[*Sunday, 5th November*]

Up early. Parade service in YMCA Cinema. Saw Agar of Winchester, leading in to the Cinema among the London Scottish.

Afternoon – went down to Harfleur Church, fine columns in interior, otherwise disappointing. A glorious exterior with crocheted spire which dominates the valley. A ride on the tramcar step to Havre, ignoring the expostulations of the conductor from within the crowded car. Ignorance of a language has its occasional advantages! Cafe au lait in a patisserie took me back to years ago though the uniform brings one different treatment from of yore – always kindly, but at times extortionate. A round of the shops and the purchases of 'unde' for M's birthday. Again cafe au – no – 'Il n'y a plus du lait' so cafe noir suffices. Talked with a Canadian, educated at St Paul's School, who is a member of the Pioneer Battalion. He advises me to give preference to the Pioneers and not try to transfer to the infantry.

More rain as I return to camp and a heavy downpour later.

[*Monday, 6th November*]

'Interior Economy' day. Sew on buttons, darn socks – for the first time and with much pride in the result – only a small hole as a first test. Received cake by post, a real touch of home. Spent afternoon writing letters. Good luck to-day – six letters and two newspapers to hand.

[*Tuesday, 7th November*]

'Up the hill' to parade ground as usual. Pouring rain on arrival and we march back more or less wet to Cinema for lectures. Afternoon quietly spent in reading 'Manual of Field Engineering'. Feeling of exalted virtue after such an effort! Tried to trace Major H.F. Chinney, Old Shirburnian, and at last learned his address at Headquarters, Director of Communications. Heavy rain at night and in the evening.

[*Wednesday, 8th November*]

M's birthday, also Tom's. Told off for Beach fatigue. Two sergeants, 12 men, 4 drivers and 8 mules with 4 wagons leave at 7.30 for sea shore. Duty is to pick four loads of pebbles for camp road making. We rattle down over the cobbled roads and get to work on the beach, walking back over five miles for dinner. Ride down again in afternoon through heavy rainstorms and load up again in double quick time. Take tram back in time for tea. Heavy rain and distant thunderstorm in evening.

Met new corporals and several men from 24th Battalion. Heard that Sgt Price was shot through the kidneys and Sgt Green had a machine-

13

gun bullet through his helmet, leaving him unhurt. Tremendous thunderstorm and floods of rain at night. Kept dry.

[*Thursday, 9th November*]

'Up the hill' as usual and spent the day in a dugout 42ft deep in charge of party at work of enlargement. Soil a rich red rock sand, the only trouble is caused by rain which descended the two stairways from the flooded trenches the previous evening. This was bailed into empty oil cans and passed up the stairs in reliefs; after that the work was easier. Progress was slow as all earth excavated had to be passed up in sandbags. In charge of the work was a Durham miner as instructor and his business-like pick strokes were a marvel to the uninitiated. Rain at times during the day.

[*Friday, 10th November*]

Once more 'up the hill' for final work. On musketry all day. Warned for draft to leave Saturday night. Fine bright day and very mild.

[*Saturday, 11th November*]

Draft paraded in morning but told off for 17th Battalion. Therefore, Sgt Wilson, myself and Cpl Martin are taken out of the draft and will go up later to the 20th Battalion. Am warned later to conduct the draft 'up the line'. Parade in the dark in full marching order with rifle but no ammunition, and have to report to 2nd Lt Crowdy, RFA.[3] Each man has received a pair of trench gloves, a shrapnel helmet[4] worn for the present in the middle of the back, all adding to the weight of a burdensome pack – and 120 rounds of ammunition. A brief inspection in the dark, a few words from the Chaplain on 'steadfastness' and the draft moved off – no fuss, no ceremony, no band. Many other detachments from other camps make up a long column.

Away we march in a drizzly mist which adds to the prevailing darkness. We take the lower road to Havre and trudge along with steady tramp down the muddy roads, at times stepping up to our ankles in slush as an earnest of more in store in coming trench life. We pass huge factories in full work, the Canadian camp, the German prison camp heavily wired and guarded.

With one brief halt in the five miles march we reach the entraining shed at Le Havre station. Here the first duty is the issue of two days'

---

[3] Royal Field Artillery.
[4] Steel helmets were introduced for the first time in the British Army in February 1916 (*Official History of the Ministry of Munitions*).

rations per man, and an iron ration for one day – which no man is allowed to touch without an officer's special order. In our party are four corporals who take over the work of issuing the iron rations in the railway van and of doling out cheese, bully beef, biscuits, jam, tea and sugar to the men.

The transport officer chalks off the waiting carriages for the various regiments and we find ourselves in luck. 27 men go into three compartments of an ordinary coach; the remaining 55 and myself are told off to one large corridor carriage. The men settle down comfortably enough in 8s and 6s in the carriages, and I choose a full length couch in the corridor with waterproof sheet for mattress, valise for pillow and overcoat for covering. The huge train moved off about 11 p.m. and from 11.30 to 5.30 a.m. I slept soundly and well. Then I woke to hear the morning chimes of the bells of Rouen. It was but 5.30 and the train moved on slowly across the river Seine and came to a halt in the large entraining shed.

Here we stayed for more than an hour and at last got the word to fall in on the platform. Then we marched off under the guidance of a Canadian artillery officer to the rest camp. Rations of two days tea and sugar and milk were given out and then I had time for a visit to the canteen and the purchase of postcards. These I found the Chaplain would censor and later he was good as his word. A short service in the canteen and hearty singing by the men with an earnest address by the Chaplain – lately come from Thiepval – on the stern [discipline] of self-sacrifice at the present time, contrasted with the easy pleasant life of three years ago! As a prayer the men all impressively repeated the hymn for absent friends. That is the Christian presentation of the virtues of war. The other side shows itself in the instructors' biddings to take no prisoners and to provide as many as possible strange faces in Hell and those not English. As a military necessity the killing of all men found in the front-line trenches is sound and probably salutary. It also carries out the Bismarckian doctrine of making war terrible, as the Franctireurs found to their cost in 1870.

At 12.50 all fell in again and marched to the station waiting for the train to be marked off for them. This time our luck was out. For the 83 men of the 17th KRR there were two closed-in cattle or horse trucks, to hold forty apiece, and three places in a similar truck for the sergeant (myself) and two lance corporals. Each bunk is boarded and the sides painted. Beyond a few nails and screws in the walls there is no furniture whatsoever. With some signs of dissent the men settle down amid strange surroundings. There is just sitting room for all but with legs cramped close up, and so the journey begins – about 3 p.m.

We jog along in leisurely fashion with many a wayside halt and at the end of three hours find ourselves 10 miles from Rouen, our starting point. The journey is not without interest. The side doors of the trucks are open and men sit in the doorway swinging their legs.

Soon it gets dark, the doors are closed, and we sit down and finally stretch out as far as we can, for rest at full length is rarely possible. Slowly and with frequent halts we rumble on through the night.

Next morning we halt for two hours or more at Abbeville. On we got until Doullens is reached. Here came word down the train that there would be a 'halt of half an hour'. Fully one hundred men stream across to the little canteen which is crowded to the doors. Suddenly there is a cry 'She's off' and turning round we see the train going off at high speed! There is a mad rush and scramble across the rails. Unfortunately there is another train covering the greater length of the one in motion. So the avenue of approach is narrow. Men climb into the carriages, throw themselves onto the buffers, or swing on to a small goods truck in rear and scramble along the roofs. Two men lose their grasp and fall from the moving train and spin round as they roll on the ground safe! As the train steamed out thirty men stream wildly after it, expecting each moment it will pull up and let them get on board. No! The chase goes on for half a mile. Then a wayside sergeant – for I was among the missing – [tells us] to persevere to the next station 5 kilometres and there we shall catch it up. We follow along the track until a gendarme with pointed bayonet turns us onto the high road. A brisk walk, with an occasional trot, and Gezaincourt is reached.

As we pass through the village the whistle blows and the train is off again! We rush once more and follow some way along the track, knowing how frequently a train halts just after leaving a station. Our luck is out and regretfully we report to the RTO.[5] (Others of our party, missing the road to Gezaincourt, find themselves at Candas, and are lucky enough to catch the train there.) The RTO advises that a train will come in for us in 'twenty minutes' time'. We wait for 1¾ hours and our chances are gone! Truly our luck is out!

At Candas we catch a horse train, reach Varennes about 10.30, walk down to Acheux only to find that draft has not arrived. Soon Sgt Wilson with 2nd Batt. draft comes in and I learn that my draft has detrained at Varennes! I am told by the RTO that a guide will conduct the party to the 39th Division next morning.

Retire to rest but with no windows or doors. With water bottles as pillow I lie down and sleep on bare boards.

From Doullens onwards we have heard the incessant boom of heavy guns, and a stream of hospital trains is going down to the base at Acheux. We are much nearer to the firing and the hut shakes and rattles with the vibration. There are 1,500 prisoners near by in a concentration

[5] Railway Transport Officer.

camp. The wind is keen and at 3.15 I wake, too cold to sleep. Getting up I go to Varennes, hoping to get news of the draft. This is not forthcoming except that the empty train stands in the station. I return to Acheux to find a guide and after much enquiry find that there is none there.

Off to Varennes again, and at last I learn that the draft has moved off to Hedouville. On to Bougaincourt in search of Headquarters of 39th Division, and up to Northumberland Avenue this is found. Then on, more kilometres towards bridge to Martin Saint. At Bougaincourt I entered the area of war desolation. Houses breached and pock-marked by shell-fire, windows broken and roofs shattered. The distant spire of Albert Church hangs down dismally like the broken bough of a tree. The British lines are now about five miles distant, the flash of guns and the burst of enemy shells is plainly visible. Firing goes on unceasingly, columns of men are going up towards the trenches and several streams of prisoners are being shepherded to the rear. I dip into a valley and climb to a ridge nearer to the enemy where I find the 17th KRR. The draft (12.30 p.m.) has not yet arrived. Dine with CQMSs[6] of battalion.

Imagine a village the size of Twyford. The church shell marked, windows broken, tower stripped of slates, churchyard entrenched. Farm houses given over to billets for troops, mud everywhere, no glass remaining. No animal life remaining except for the faithful pigeons on the church tower. Desolation everywhere. Little food to be procured in the village, so bully beef and biscuits are the rule. From here the men go up to the trenches, the lines of which are plainer at night outlined by the star shells.

At 3 p.m. the draft arrives and I am duly 'strafed' by the officer! My kit he says has 'gone to hell' left at the Brigade Divisional Ammunition Dump – which does not sound promising! After seeing the Quartermaster I set out to find the pack and for three solid hours carry on a vain pursuit amid all the 'dumps' in the neighbourhood.

I return to Martin Saint to find the whole Brigade moving on to Warloi, where the QMS[7] tells me I may recover my belongings. We leave at 9.30 p.m. on foot, and in charge of five shoemakers! A lift on a motor lorry helps us on our way, but it is 12.30 a.m. before we reach camp. The main body and transport have not arrived and empty tents await us. I stroll up and down under the stars. The bombardment has livened up with the rising of the moon and there is plenty to see and hear.

A sound of an aeroplane is heard and as I was admiring the daring of our night airmen, suddenly – Whoof! Bang! Bang! A couple of bombs

[6] Company Quartermaster Sergeants.
[7] Quartermaster Sergeants.

fell in the camp not fifty yards from where I was standing but clear of the tent. A fatigue party had a narrow escape but no one was hurt.

[*Wednesday, 15th November*]

Up in the sky there is a sound of 'Tack – Tick-a-tick-tack' as the machine gun of a British aeroplane is turned on the invader. There is a battle in progress for several minutes, the two are parted, and return to the attack again. Another British aeroplane arrives and the invader is driven off and the British patrols sail round and round shewing a pair of tail lights.

The column come in at 8 a.m. and we settle down to sleep. I am wrapped in a rubber sheet and sleep thus to seven o'clock. I search the whole camp for my kit without success, report to Adjutant and another strafing. Then off to the rail head and the journey home.

Arrive at Varennes at 10 a.m. No train until 4.10 p.m. Set off by road for Doullens, 24 kilometres distant. By this time the heels of my only pair of socks are gone and I am glad of the lift or two from friendly lorries. Arrive at Doullens at 1.30 and spend quiet afternoon in quaint little country town. Leave Doullens 9 p.m. in 2nd class carriage and reach Abbeville at 3 a.m.

[*Thursday, 16th November*]

Found the YMCA hut where the men are walking round and round in single file, as it is too cold to sleep. I lie down but soon follow the procession of other men. Breakfast, and then fall in with Sgt Wilson who was in a later train down from Doullens. A good wash and shave with borrowed razor and we go out together into the town.

A splendid exterior to Abbey and a quaint town unspoilt by modern building. It is market day and many are the round hooded carts laid up near by. Dejourner [sic] at a market cafe and enjoy a quiet day. It is cold with sharp frost in early morning. I miss my overcoat but have lined trousers, chest and back with paper. The military police are active and hands in pockets are against the rule. In the afternoon we stroll again, watch an English football match, taste a bag of chips freshly fried by an old dame who draws all her customers into conversation, and my halting French is aired at frequent intervals during the day.

We are due at railway station at 6 p.m. At 9 p.m. no Havre train has arrived and we enter a goods truck and keep as warm as we can with a biscuit tin brazier filled with coke.

11.30. At last a train is made up. I lie down under blankets again, the first time for nearly a week, for a friendly ASC man lets me share

18

Somewhere on the Western Front.

his. A cattle truck again, but clean and nearly new. Slept soundly til 8 a.m.

[*Friday, 17th November*]

Wake up to a hard frost and to find that we have almost reached Dieppe! Move on slowly with frequent halts that do not even arouse curiosity. Time is no object on this train! It seems the French authorities have handed over a part of the various stations to the British, and grant them two trains a day for the movement of troops. My offer to pay my own fare and travel by ordinary train evoked this explanation. No British troops travel by French trains. A long halt. I run along the track to the engine with billy can, and tea is made by a turn of the friendly driver's tap.

We pass Neuchatel-en-Bray. Halts become more frequent than ever. By this time we have grasped the sober truth that we are classed as 'Returned empties' – too true in *my* case – and are shunted and left by the trackside accordingly!

Reach Serquel. Remain for several hours just outside Rouen. Once clear of that town we make fair speed for Le Havre. Get out at Harfleur with snow on the ground. Reach camp – with my faithful water bottle as my only kit at 3 a.m.

[Saturday, 18th November]

Lay in bed until 10 a.m. Reported to Orderly Sgt my loss of kit and rifle and had an interview with Sgt-Major. Am to appear before the Colonel at Orderly Room in morning.

[Sunday, 19th November]

Appeared before Colonel who tells me to put in a written statement. Warned for draft for following day.

[Monday, 20th November]

Appear before Colonel who goes through my statement sentence by sentence, and wants to know 'What wonderful condition I am in', to expect to catch up a train which has steamed out of the station! He also asked me if I had covered the distance I traversed on foot, and said I had done all I possibly could under the circumstances. If my story on investigation should prove to be true the new kit issued to me would not be charged against me. Much relieved, and prepare with a light heart to go off on draft to the 20th Battalion at Mailley-Mallet – thus repeating my journey of last week.

Packing kit and fitting up my new equipment all the afternoon. Parade at 6.30, a brief address from the Colonel on the responsibility of our task, and a few words from the Chaplain. We move off with a few handshakes and words of farewell – no cheering as departure of drafts is an everyday event.

A clear starlit night, a heavy pack and much mud under foot as we move off on our five-mile tramp to Le Havre. We are a party of 17 for the 20th Battalion. Sgt William in charge, Sgt Travers, an Australian previously wounded with 20th Battalion, Sgt Wardman, blacksmith, and Corporal Martin previously wounded with 20th Battalion.

Entrain at Le Havre and travel fairly to Rouen where we spend the morning in the rest camp.

[Tuesday, 21st November]

Conditions here are not new to me. A short service by the Chaplain in which the men join heartily. Join train at 3 p.m. and leave for Abbeville arriving at 4 a.m. Travel 32 in a small horse carriage, an uncomfortable night sitting up in a cramped position.

October 1916 to February 1917: The Somme

[*Wednesday, 22nd November*]
Officer declares that train may move off at any minute. In view of my previous week's experience I remain faithfully near the railway van – until 3 p.m. Move off slowly to Fourtel, 55 minutes, where we come to a halt at a little wayside station and are told that we remain there probably for the night. Canadian artillery men make a raid on boxes of eggs and also upon estaminet, so a guard of twelve men prevent all from leaving the station. The men make a number of small fires on the platform by the side of the train, fed by portions of the station fence and coke from the goods yard! Here tea is made and food cooked. A large loaf of bread which I brought from Rouen proves most useful.

Settle down early for the night and so secure lying-down room. Interludes of discomfort through men kicking out, and much laughter caused thereby. Some men are champion grumblers. Sleep soundly towards morning.

[*Thursday, 23rd November*]
Get water from station well and shave with an apology for a wash. Sgt Wilson and Cpl Martin move off down the village for breakfast. We move off about 9.15 and the two are left behind. At Doullens another day's rations are issued. We move on very slowly.

A lovely sunny day after a frosty night. A few leaves still on the topmost branches of the trees. A long wait before reaching Gandas. More diversions by Canadians who set out to milk the cows in the fields near by! Milk and one Canadian knocked over by one cow! Names of all concerned are taken down by an officer. Undismayed one Canadian crosses the path of a white hen which he promptly beheads and brings back under his arm.

Slowly the train drifts on with several other long trains drawn up in rear, others in front. Darkness comes on. About 8 p.m. we reach a place which proves to be Belle Eglise. We detrain all in pitch darkness and stumble across a field lined with ditches into one of which Sgt Travers stumbles knee deep. We are shown into a big marquee set up in a slimy field and lie down on our useful waterproof sheets with the water oozing up underneath.

[*Friday, 24th November*]
Wake up to a fine morning. There is a German prisoners' camp in the next field. Our guide is ready about 9 a.m. and we march off fully loaded. Roads are execrable and progress is slow. For myself, a pair of new boots do not make things easier. We have frequent rests and about 12 o'clock have reached our destination, the village of Courcelles.

21

It is a typical little country place centred round four cross-roads and the village church which has suffered less than many near by. The village has suffered from shell fire and there are many shattered buildings and shrapnel-pitted walls. Roads are rivers of mud and bear much heavy traffic for which they were never built.

We present ourselves at the Orderly Room – the dwelling house of a small farmstead near the church, and I am allotted to 'C' Company. As conducted by the Orderly Sgt to my quarters where I find the Company Sgt's Mess a little outhouse of corrugated iron with a coke brazier in the centre of an earthen floor which is covered with trench boards. Round the stove are seated about a dozen sergeants at their mid-day meal to which they make me welcome. A place is allotted to me in the far corner opposite the door, and I settle down agreeably surprised at the snugness of my new home.

Outside are a number of dilapidated out-buildings, a dungheap in the foreground, for the stables are in use, and a filthy little pond leading to the garden of which only a few sad fruit trees remain. I receive orders to go up with the troops on wiring work in front of the support trenches. We are to start at 3 a.m. so I lie down to rest as much as strong coke fumes will allow.

About 9 p.m. I am warned to parade at the Orderly Room in the morning and not to go to the trenches. It is now raining hard and I am not altogether sorry. Sleep heavily and wake up in the morning with a heavy head and a feeling of being drugged – the effects of a coke fire.

[*Saturday, 25th November*]
Go to Orderly Room for brief interview with the CO, Major Ingles. Return to our Mess and spend rest of the day lying on the floor out of the rain. The weather is misty and there are few guns booming. Receive orders to go up to the trenches for wiring work: reveille 2.15, breakfast 2.45, parade 3.15 a.m. To 'bed' early.

[*Sunday, 26th November*][8]
My first day on trench work! More pouring rain all the evening and during the night. Woke at 1.30 when rain was pouring down. Lay abed wondering until 2.15. Meanwhile the orderly man is lighting the fire and fries some bacon. The rain had ceased by the time we had had a hasty breakfast and the stars were shining brightly by the time the company 'fell in' outside Headquarters. The village road was half

---

[8] The Battle of the Somme has been officially over for five days. Many of Warren's sister battalions – particularly the 16th, 10th and 21st KRRC – have taken part and have suffered severe casualties.

covered with water. We march off up the village to the north, over the worn and shell-torn road to Colincamps, a village shattered beyond repair by the conflicting armies. Thence we follow a road track and a light railway behind the line of the British reserve trenches. It is pitch dark and cloudy now, so stumble along, falling into shell holes full of water, and thanking Fritz whenever a star shell went up. One unfortunate man fell into a shell-hole up to his neck in water.

There is an approach by way of a trench but our officer knowing this to be very watery decides on continuing 'on top' and we advance by way of the track. Our objective is reached; pickets and wire are drawn from the dump. The men had previously been told off to their tasks and at once set out the screw-in iron picquets, fixing them lightly in the ground. These iron uprights or stakes are then screwed in by another set of men cork-screw fashion, until they are two feet or more in the ground. The long picquets are set out in the old quincunx fashion, which gave solidity to the Roman cohort; the pattern is represented in modern style by a five of diamonds. To these strands of wire are laced top and bottom, in and out, until a fine tangle is evolved. Then loose strands are flung in and fixed here and there. More picquets, shorter this time, are laid outside the original three and trip and apron wires are set up.

By the time all this could be seen and the work was done, it had long been daylight, and we had been wondering what Fritz had been thinking of it all on the ridge over to the right, probably 1,000 yards distant. We had been working for some hours and there was no cover. British shells had been going over at intervals all night and had become more frequent as daylight broke. Fritz gave no answer.

We were sent into the trench, up to the top of our boots in water, whilst the officer inspected the work. We were told to come out of the trench. The officer wanted an extra bit done beyond our task. We set to with a few grumbles but with a haste which promised an early finish. This proved to be the case. By 8.15 we had finished and Fritz had not woken up. It had rained hard from the moment we had begun wiring, a keen wind was blowing and all were chilled to the bone. We decide upon the road 'over the top' once more as the rain seemed to have hidden us from Fritz's view. We hurry home to get some warmth into our bones.

As we approach Colincamps the British 'heavies' open out freely, and we hurry on expecting a reply on the open road on which we are strung out. No reply came. When we reach camp we hear the rumour that Fritz has been flooded out of his first and second line trenches and has moved back to his third line of defence. However that might be, there is much water about and the British heavies are extra busy all day. As

23

I write the wall bulges and things fall from the walls with each heavy discharge from a place nearby.

I am reduced to an overcoat and a pair of pants until I can dry off my clothes, but sit warmly in my only blanket, and welcome the coke brazier now. I learn that our wiring was done in advance of Sackville Street, now our reserve line trench, as Rob Roy is said to be full of water. Spend rest of the day in resting, cleaning up and go early to bed. A second blanket issued to each man.

[*Monday, 27th November*]

Reveille at 2.45. Was sleeping heavily when roused at 3.10. Had to dress hastily; have a breakfast of brawn, bread, butter and jam. Fall in at 3.50, a fine, frosty morning, but only the surface frozen. There was almost as much slush as ever afoot. Our work today was wiring in front of Southern Avenue trench, near the spot where a British aeroplane was brought down by the enemy.

Here the boys got to work, though the numbers were much fewer owing to sick absentees. The place is freely pitted with shell-holes; the trenches were formerly German, so they have the range to a nicety. As daylight draws on the work proceeds well. A fine view of the bend in the German lines is seen from the high ground here. The British line here presents a salient, but Fritz has successfully thrown back further attempts to advance.

A glorious and sunny morning with a light mist. Home by 8.45. Rest and write letters. Receive first letters from home and a parcel (Balaclava cap, mittens, and scarf the work of my dear wife, God bless her!) and a cake from Ethel Beaven. Was in 'bed' by 7 p.m. Slept soundly.

[*Tuesday, 28th November*]

A fine frosty morning, but not keen enough to consolidate the roads. Our work was again in front of Southern Avenue. A thick mist rising towards daybreak made the conditions ideal for our work and a lot of progress was made. Fritz again very quiet.

As we returned the guns of the batteries of Southern Avenue trench opened up as we passed their front, and we were almost stunned by the explosion not thirty yards away. On return made a detour round Colincamps as our guns were 'strafing' Fritz heavily and his reply would probably fall on village road. Much mud in the fields.

A good wash in hot water and feel much more comfortable. Rest and write letters. A good fire going in the brazier all the morning. Have Woodborough cake for tea – much appreciated.

To bed at 7 p.m. after rubbing whale oil on feet. Slept well.

[*Wednesday, 29th November*]

Up at 2.45, fall in at 3.20 and march to wire. Redoubt near Southern Avenue trench. Again foggy with a slight touch of frost. Returned 9 a.m. Fritz has begun to busy himself and there is a number of new shell-holes about. As I write after breakfast Fritz is sending over a dozen or so shrapnel shells in the neighbourhood. More shelling later in the morning and a few fall on the outskirts of Courcelles.

Received a letter from Harold Stratton and a large tin of caramels from Tom and Meg. Slept in afternoon until teatime. Went to bed at 9 p.m.

[*Thursday, 30th November*]

Reveille at 2.45, parade 3.50. Cooks were late with breakfast; it is 4.30 before we get away. The night is the darkest we have had and we stumble along under a cloudy moonless sky. When we get through Colincamps and out into the open country Fritz's star shells and the flashes of the British guns light us on our way.

We are wiring outside Southern Avenue beyond where the old British aeroplane lies. It turns out a clear frosty morning. We can see the village of Serre, in German occupation, and an artillery officer warns us that we are under Hun observation. We receive orders to leave early and a few of No. 9 Platoon remain behind to finish off and save us a journey up the following morning.

On the way back through Colincamps we can see the damage done by last night's bombardment. Two more houses have been knocked down; four or five shells have pitched in the street; one shell has struck the church, north wall, shaken the foundations and bursting upwards has turned back a large portion from the eaves upwards. Another has struck the church tower. There are a few new holes near Courcelles and the water-pipe outside the village has been severed. Fritz has shown some accurate shooting. Probably the reason why he did not open fire on us this morning was that he had parties out himself and did not seek retaliation.

[*Friday, 1st December*]

A quiet day and a morning in bed. Breakfast 8 a.m. Working parties out from other companies and a sergeant of 'B' Co. wounded on Rob Roy trench. Another party shelled as they stepped back into trench. A waxing moon and nights grow lighter. No mail today.

[*Saturday, 2nd December*]

On as sergeant on guard. All day in verminous little hut, about 9ft x 7ft with small annexe for six prisoners. Two men checked for dirty rifles and party called a 'ragtime' lot by the 'assistant adjutant'.

Receive three letters, two papers and a parcel from Northampton (? Gertrude Wilkes). Read first war news I have heard since Nov. 20th, and that under date Nov. 25th. Sit all day on uncomfortable plank and balance at full length for an hour or two at night. Feel creepy all over after contact with mud walls.

[*Sunday, 3rd December*]

Another strange Sunday in this seven work day week! Came off guard at 9 a.m. A good wash to the waist and sorted out clothes for the wash, hoping to escape the general plague even after 24 hours in the mud-built guardroom. Miss the home comforts as I am resting today. A nicely warmed room with plenty of vases of English flowers and fresh faces and voices would be a welcome change, especially on a Sunday. Yet this life has its interests, and after all it is but a stopgap.

About 10 p.m. a serious mishap in the village behind the church. A premature explosion of a 9.2mm shell killed or wounded a dozen men (3 killed and 9 wounded). Several men were in the road and the gunners also suffered. Part of the roof of No. 9 Platoon billets was carried away by a fragment of the shell.

[*Monday, 4th December*]

A pitch dark night after the moon had set. Reveille at 2.45. Breakfast, and set out to bring down the platoon to Headquarters. So dark that I missed the turning and floundered about in a ditch before retracing my steps and getting on the right track. Moist under foot, but as we reach the open country it is freezing hard and the ground stiffens.

We are wiring near Waterloo Bridge behind our recent line of wire. The work is to repair smashed up French wire, and the job is finished by 7.30, home by 8.30. A lovely morning and we can look right away to the line of gaunt tree stumps which denotes Serre. We do not wait long as there is little mist to hide us.

Rest until dinnertime, then witness the chasing of a Taube,[9] several of which have been very daring today. Does this mean shelling for us tonight?

---

[9] British troops called all German aeroplanes 'Taubes' in the early part of the war.

We went out as usual at 4 a.m. Not such blank darkness this morning, and Fritz was sending up more flares than usual. We crossed Southern Avenue trench by way of Waterloo Bridge and went down to work on some old wire beyond the damaged aeroplane and over the narrow gauge railway.

We had been working half an hour or so when the British batteries opened up heavily in the direction of Serre. This seemed to stir up Fritz who began to reply, and in our direction! There was the scream of a shell and the curious diminuendo which showed it to be approaching. Plonk! It had pitched and exploded over the hedge on Southern Avenue trench, behind the spot where No. 10 Platoon was working – a little lower down than we were.

More shells followed getting uncomfortably nearer, and for the first time I was under shell-fire. It must be owned that my knees shook a bit! But I found that I had full control of my voice and carried on with the direction of the work for a few minutes. More shells, and I found myself ducking, as others were doing, in anticipation of each explosion. There was a call for stretcher-bearers, and a man of No. 10 Platoon was brought along by two others groaning loudly. This did not improve matters.

Sgt Maybank in charge of No. 9 Platoon gave the order to retire to the trench, and if the truth be told I was not sorry to hear it. I waited to see the last man of the platoon clear of the work, for several of them had mislaid their rifles. Next I heard the officer of No. 11 telling No. 9 to return to their work and I turned back. I got back to the wire again and only three men were with me. After making enquiries I found that after all No. 9 had been ordered to retire to Southern Avenue trench, and thither I followed them.

We waited in the trench for a time and then received orders to make for the dugouts, which we did, for the shells were still coming over. Daylight came and we received orders to go back and finish our work as the shelling had ceased. When I left off work I was standing by the dump counting out short pickets. When we returned we found a big shell-hole (hole about six feet across and three feet deep) on the spot where I had been standing and another ten yards away, just the other side of the narrow gauge railway. The shelling was probably from a single gun (5.9in) which was searching the trench line, or putting up a barrage against the approach of troops. It could not be called a heavy bombardment but it was a novelty for me.

The man Brown who screamed and groaned returned to his company headquarters unhurt! He was then placed under arrest for leaving the trenches without permission.

Rain came on shortly after our return to our quarters. Slept all the afternoon. In the evening cake and walnuts arrived from Madge. British guns were busy in quarter of an hour bursts. I hear that eight of our men died as the result of the premature bursting of a shell as already recorded.

No letter received direct from home since I reached this place, only a letter or two and a parcel via Havre.

[*Wednesday, 6th December*]

Up to Waterloo Bridge and wiring in the same spot as yesterday. British batteries very busy as we get to work patching up the old wire as a third line of defence. British machine gun busy on our right where also Fritz was sending over some shells, searching for our batteries. But none came our way.

Returned home by 8.45. As we came out of Colincamps a big shell burst, away on our right. A foggy morning, and we could not have been seen from the German lines today.

On my return had a bath, really hot, and a change of clothes. Can congratulate myself on avoiding vermin up to the present time.

[*Thursday, 7th December*]

Reveille 2 a.m., parade at 3.30; Sgt Maybank was allowed a rest so I went up in charge of the platoon for the first time.

Wiring work was a third line of wire just in front of La Signy farm. Moonlight as we went up, but when moon went down it was very dark until dawn at about 6.30. With two good corporals (Cpls David and Bainbridge) to set out the pickets and start the wiring, all went well and our job of about 90 yards went on swimmingly.

Towards the finish the officer (Mr Williams) borrowed six men to help out No. 10 Platoon with their work. It was a very cold morning. Fritz was throwing over shells at regular intervals, but all passed over our heads or away to the right.

When we got home about 9.30 a.m. we learned that two men of 'A' Company had been hit – a corporal and a lance corporal – both hit in the arm.

Spent the morning asleep and did not even trouble to shave – my first time of missing this, but I was tired out. It is now six o'clock and our guns have opened out heavily against Fritz.

No letter from home since Saturday and that one posted via Le Havre. Am wondering when first letter from home will reach me. Good luck! The post has just brought me a letter from home, again via Le Havre, and also an oilskin silk waistcoat with sleeves from Clifton and which I afterwards learned was a Christmas present from Harold.

[*Friday, 8th December*]

Out by 3.50 a.m. More moonlight at first, but rain later. Fritz was sending over some trench mortars to the right of La Signy Farm, where we were working.

Arrived home about 9 a.m. Washed, shaved and slept. For dinner had a plum duff, the first pudding we have seen since our arrival. Rested all afternoon. Three letters arrived in evening.

[*Saturday, 9th December*]

Slept the clock round and awoke refreshed. Wrote a 'green envelope' letter[10] home. Pouring rain all day. Tomorrow night we go up to front-line trenches for wiring. After tea a singsong and all much refreshed by night and day's rest!

[*Sunday, 10th December*]

Awoke at 8 a.m. after a good night's rest. Found the yard outside our hut a miniature lake after the heavy rain. Paraded the platoon to make a list of the deficiencies in kit. The shortage of socks is a scandal, seeing that men get wet feet every night, and on their return have no change and only a wornout pair on their feet. Wrote home to Maud to ask if the Mayoress of Winchester or the KRR fund could spare any socks.

After tea a singsong round the coke brazier. Fell in at 9 p.m. to go up to Nairn trench in our front line to put up a third line of wire – in front of the two already in position. Almost a full moon with a thin haze of cloud which left us a good working light but threw no betraying shadows. Left the village past the windmill and took to the turf tracks almost at once, thus avoiding Colincamps, which as events proved was freely shelled by the Germans. The heavy rains of the previous two days had turned all tracks into quagmires, and soon we were floundering more than ankle deep.

So we went on, past some of our batteries which at intervals were spitting shrapnel at any spot where Fritz chose to show a magnesium light. All the while our 'heavies' were sending over their big shells with their railroad scream and flash of light as they cut through the thin clouds above us. Such noise as we made could not have been heard to our disadvantage, for rarely were there a few seconds of silence by reason of the roar of the guns, and a gentle breeze was blowing down to us from the German lines on our right – and across our front as far as our enemies on the left were concerned. Here the British line presents

---

[10] A limited number of 'green envelopes' were issued to troops – these letters would not be opened or censored.

a salient so that the Hun flares could be seen directly on our right and our left.

Our material was brought up to us by a Line battalion to the head of our light railway, and thence had to be carried half a mile up hill and over the most treacherous ground and broken trenches. As we drew near our allotted spot we found ourselves fortunately below the skyline. Each of three platoons quickly and quietly got to work on our scheme of work. The drawback was that when the first material was used up, the work stood still until more could be got from the dump. When they arrived all was finished up in a way that drew warm praises from the officers.

About 2 a.m. we left our 'home' by way of Northern Avenue trench. The mud was even worse than on our upward journey and we were often over the tops of our boots. Had we gone by way of the trenches themselves I know not what it might have been like! In our retirement we probably showed ourselves on the skyline, for Fritz began to turn his shrapnel in our direction. Fortunately he placed it well away to our left just below the further side of the ridge on which we were travelling. We pushed on quickly, for the clouds had now passed off the face of the moon.

Five minutes after we passed La Signy Farm Fritz turned his aim directly upon our track, but perhaps 200 yards to the rear was the nearest explosion. This was enough to make us hasten our pace. In one place a trench not more than three feet had to be crossed. One man kept all others back by refusing to cross. I came up to him and said: 'Jump, man, jump!' His reply was 'I can't, Sergeant, my pants are coming down!' But he had to jump! From that time we began to get clear of German shells, but not of the mud. That was a minor item. The main thing was that all returned safely by 4 a.m. for an early breakfast. 'A' Company who had returned before us had had two casualties, both slight, one in the hand and one in the arm. For the day we rested (Monday).

[Tuesday, 12th December]
Snow on the ground when we woke in the morning and as it thawed our quarters were nearly flooded, and a river of water flowed past our doors. In the afternoon we received orders to move our quarters to another part of the village, near the RE[11] dump. It was nearly dark before we received definite orders. When we reached our new rooms we found a mud-walled hut, no door, no windows, puddles on the floor, a leaky roof and little encouragement for newcomers! Trench boards on

[11] Royal Engineers.

30

the floor, a good fire burning in the brazier made the place more cheerful. We settled down to rest, and soon the rats made their presence known. They performed gymnastics on the wall by my side, and finally dropped on to me and played about the floor beneath my pillow.

[*Wednesday, 13th December*]

Woke up cold in the morning, breakfast in bed, and wrote letters and read all day.

8 p.m. Sitting in our quarters whilst Fritz is shelling the village. Shells fall at one minute intervals and fragments of shell and dirt are clattering on the roof. Once he shook the whole building with a shell just at the back. We left our quarters for a few minutes with our shrapnel helmets on our heads, but the next shell was further away and we returned to bed. About a dozen shells fell mainly on the road and were probably fired from an armoured train.

Asleep by 9 p.m. and on waking was told that Fritz had put up another bombardment, and again fragments were falling around us. No casualties occurred, although a shed was levelled to the ground at the back of the Orderly Room. By the Colonel's orders the guard was told to scatter, and guard and prisoners seven might have been seen bolting in different directions!

[*Thursday, 14th December*]

Reveille at 2.30, set off at 3.30 a.m. Much water on the roads but fair moonlight. Led up to Euston Camp, past the ruins of the Sugar Refinery, on the Serre road past Taupin trench. Some of the platoon were away on guard and the work went slowly. About 8 a.m. we were on our way homeward and nearing Colincamps. Down the road was coming an Artillery officer. As he passed I suddenly recognised a familiar face, and called out, 'Phil Hart!' He looked surprised and said, 'And who are you?' I said, 'Frank Warren' and he then welcomed me warmly and walked back up the road with me. He told me that he was observation officer in front of Taupin trench and enquired of my whereabouts. He was looking well, almost sleek, and thoroughly happy in his work.

Rested for remainder of day. Received orders to fall in at 9 p.m. for another wiring expedition. We set off by way of the fields, as Fritz had been sending his 'crumps' during the day into Colincamps. Almost at once we were wallowing in mud and progress was slow and very tiring.

[*Friday, 15th December*]

We reached our destination about 1.30 a.m. after taking an hour to cross Jean Bart trench, dug very deep and wide and almost knee deep in slush. Wire coils had also to be thrown across. We had to throw loose wire across the unfinished work of another Battalion. This did not take very long. Fritz was throwing shrapnel about but not dangerously near. We were not home until 4 a.m. thoroughly tired.

After resting up to 2 p.m. six of us sergeants set out to replenish our wood supplies, as there is no comfort without a fire. We took a hand-cart and took our way to Colincamps. Went into church which was surprisingly undamaged considering the sad state of the exterior. Opposite found a huge beam which two of us moved but could not shoulder. Dyke came to the rescue and we raised it shoulder high, staggering through the mud to the roadway. Then we dragged a fine broken gate from the edge of the pond and that made some good spars.

Meanwhile Thistleton had visited a house further down the road. We heard a crash. He had laid hold of a beam in the wall, and down came wall, roof and chimney! Then we had enough wood and to spare. We made a merry journey home, in spite of fearful holes in the roads. Fortunately the wheels of the truck held up, and we came home in triumph with our load, and the fire burned brightly for several days.

Fell in at 11 p.m. for another wiring expedition.

[*Saturday, 16th December*]

Reached our post in front of Jean Bart trench about 1.30 a.m. and set to work on filling in loose wire on and over 'French wire' entanglement. Fritz sent over half a dozen 'whiz-bangs' a bit to our left which made us a bit fidgety as he had the range to a nicety. Then came one just fifty yards to our rear and mud and pebbles came rattling on our helmets. Fortunately that was the last, and the work was soon finished.

We made our way home, dragging tired feet, and arrived at 5.30 a.m. Slept until 1.30 p.m., then dinner and in afternoon wrote letters and read. Several parcels from home. Went to Red Cross Corporal and got a dressing for a blistered right heel which showed signs of festering.

[*Sunday, 17th December*]

Slept well, in spite of a wet-footed rat which leapt on to my face in the middle of the night. Breakfast at 8 a.m. Ready for a parade at 10.30 a.m. Rested for the remainder of the day. More parcels came to hand. Heavy shelling and drum fire by British artillery, no doubt in support of French offensive round Verdun.

Riflemen enjoying a meal. The rum jar, marked SRD (Special Rations Department), would not normally have formed part of a meal. Regulations specified that rum had to be issued and drunk in the presence of an officer.

[*Monday, 18th December*]
We have changed our work from night wiring to trench repairs by day. Fell in at 8.20 and marched off to Southern Avenue trench. Found trench in bad condition with water well over boards. Set to work to cut channels into sump holes and soon reduced water level.

Steady flow of Hun shells all day, mostly at trench, and batteries one to two hundred yards in rear. One piece of shrapnel struck trench side six inches in front of my leg.

Returned to quarters by 4.30 tired out, for we had no mid-day ration.

[*Tuesday, 19th December*]
On trench work again at Southern Avenue. Continued the raising of trench board level and the draining of Basin Wood. Shells passing over all day long, our batteries replying vigorously.

[*Wednesday, 20th December*]
Battalion Orderly Sergeant for the day. Duties kept me [at] or near Headquarters all day.

[*Thursday, 21st December*]
Summoned to appear before the CO with a view to taking an Infantry commission. Question of age was raised, but dismissed, and a decision was postponed until I had qualified by three months service in France.

Feeling shaky and feverish all day. Had hot bath and change of clothes in afternoon. At 10.30 fell in with gum boots on and went off to Flag Avenue by way of Southern Avenue trench. Taking out slush from bottom of trench, revetting sides, and raising trench boards. Men standing and working in water all the time. Only official ration issued a mug of tea before going out and breakfast on returning at 6 a.m. Fortunately the march back to quarters restores chilled circulation.

[*Friday, 22nd December*]
Went down on to my bed on return and scarcely moved off it. Had a good night's rest though wakened by Fritz's lively bombardment of the village with two heavy guns. A few casualties so we heard in the morning.

[*Saturday, 23rd December*]
Woke up with pain in back and head and the old influenza feeling. Recovered as the day wore on. Had to report to the Quartermaster on the condition of the socks in the Platoon. Reported as follows: 'Number of men with spare socks for exchange – nil; number of men with no socks at all – 5'! Shortly after the report went in five pairs of socks reached me for distribution. The men had been making use of cap comforters and sandbags torn up and wrapped round their feet. Parcels of 3 dozen socks arrived from Maud, timely and welcome.

Went up to trenches, falling in at 10.30 p.m. A clear starlight night.

[*Sunday, 24th December*]
Returned from trenches at 6 a.m. A cold wet job, standing in water most of the time. Work consisted of baling and scooping mud and water from trench, revetting sides with angle irons and expanded wire, raising trench boards and relaying on driven pickets.

Arrived home tired and unable to eat a breakfast. Practically no food all day. Rested or slept until 'fall-in' again at 10.30 for similar work to that of the night before.

Xmas Eve, and my first Xmas morning on active service was to be spent in the trenches. We fell in at 10.30 and marched off up the Colincamps road. As we got clear of the village the sight was one never to be forgotten. The stars were shining faintly through the slight mist. Round the semi-circle of the German lines from the centre-point of which we were travelling, many of the brilliant Very lights were being sent up, their magnesium rays casting a heavy shadow even at a distance of 1,000 yards. That is a nightly occurrence though more are now in evidence than usual. Overhead a British aeroplane was travelling, and German shrapnel was bursting in the clouds around it.

Then we witnessed a sight new to all of us. In the direction of the aeroplane there was fixed up from the German lines a long strip of green lights, and another, sometimes two or three in the air at the same time. It was about 11 p.m. and our guns were rolling out salvoes and peels which gave room for few thoughts of Xmas. Was this then an answer to the proposed terms of peace? All the time we were moving quickly forward, for German heavy shrapnel was bursting behind us.

At 11.45 we were standing on Euston Dump, on high commanding ground. Xmas Day 1916, was ushered in with no message of 'Peace among men', only the railroad whistling of shells from the British Howitzers, and the steadier lonelier whispering of German shrapnel, ere it burst with a sharp crack in the rear, and a dense ball of black smoke floated away, apparently just below the cloud level.

It was now our turn to pass on the work down the trenches, an hour's walk of some difficulty, even when equipped with the orthodox waders. Work was once more at Flag Avenue, and it was a damp and chilly way of spending Xmas morning.

[*Xmas Day, 25th December*]

Arrived home at 4.30 a.m. Secured a cup of Oxo, and lying down slept until 10.45. Before turning into bed wondered if the children were yet awake, and on waking up thought of all getting ready for the service in church.

We had our sergeants' dinner at 1 p.m. Plum puddings, custard, jelly and fruit. Of myself I had had no breakfast, but was able to enjoy some dinner, laid out in our new sergeants' 'mess', a room boarded and fitted with a stovepipe. Here the sergeants spent the rest of the day in a prolonged singsong. I went to bed about 9 p.m. after having first paid a visit to the Company Sgt-Major, on his invitation.

Fritz shelled the village for some time as we lay in bed and again later in the night. Our guns had sent him over several bursts of 'hate' during the day.

[*Tuesday, 26th December*]

Boxing Day. On duty as Battalion Orderly Sgt to give me a rest from 'the line'. Attended guard-mounting and felt faint while ceremony was in progress. Went later to the doctor, but found him so busy and looking so bored that I decided he could do nothing for me. I went later to the Medical Corporal to continue dressing my blistered heel and little finger poisoned with barbed wire. Kept at my duties until 8.30 p.m. Wrote some letters of thanks for parcels.

[*Wednesday, 27th December*]

Went up in morning to Flag Avenue trench for work of revetting and laying down of trench boards. A beautiful morning and almost warm in the sun after a sharp frost. Could look out from trench and see the piles of stones and bricks – all that remains of the village of Serre. Enjoyed my work for the first time for about a week as I was feeling better. Fairly quiet day, although shells were as usual passing overhead all the while.

[*Thursday, 28th December*]

Again up at Flag Avenue trench all day. A thick damp mist floating over so that it was safe to walk about on top above the trenches. Fairly quiet day. Plenty of shells about but none coming in our trench until, just after we filed out, two pairs burst very near and we congratulated ourselves at getting well clear.

Clear morning. One of our aeroplanes shot down in front of us. Had Tom's turkey for tea. A fine meal and quite a success.

[*Friday, 29th December*]

Up at trenches (Flag Avenue) once more. A very clear day. As morning wore on Fritz began to plaster all communication trenches with shrapnel, and high explosives, sending over six or eight together at times. Fortunately none came nearer than 100 yards from us and we worked on steadily. About two o'clock he brought some shells nearer us and fragments began to fall in trench. Then two burst just in front of trench, a very shallow one only for communications, with no cover, and the officer gave the order to lead out of the trench homewards half an hour before the usual time. We found that considerable damage had been done in various parts of the trenches. Evidently Fritz had an idea that a relief of those in the trenches was going on.

[*Saturday, 30th December*]

Flag Avenue once more. Worked on steadily until about 1 p.m. when Fritz opened up with Jack Johnsons[12] and other high explosive. One shell fell on each side of trench and Sgt Spain gave the order to lead out. As we moved off, bits of shell bespattered the sides of the trench and we had a warm few minutes until we got some way up Sackville Avenue trench. From the corner where Sackville Street joins Southern Avenue trench we watched a display of Jack Johnsons bursting round the part we had just left. Earth and stones were flying 150 feet in the air and the earth fell back in waves.

Did a small amount of work in Southern Avenue and then led home. Found that Fritz had also been shelling the road and Euston Dump.

[*Sunday, 31st December*]

Owing to Fritz's mid-day activity our time of parade was changed. We now fall in at 6.50 and knock off work at 1.30 p.m. getting home at 3 p.m. A fairly quiet day. The OC Battalion sent two bottles of whisky and the CSM one bottle for the comfort of the sergeants of 'C' Company. All was cleared by the morning. I went to bed early and slept well on new wire and canvas framed mattress made by the company carpenters. Beds placed in tiers of three and I secured a top tier.

[*Monday, 1st January, 1917*]

A New Year of the war begins. Fritz had been busy in the night but a fairly quiet day. To bed early. The water in Taupin and Southern Avenue trenches which had been more than knee deep has now been pumped out. We are also now working on drier soil as water has been pumped away.

[*Tuesday, 2nd January*]

Still working in Flag Avenue. Fritz noisy about mid-day and put some close to side of trench. Watched his shells bursting all around Northern Avenue and Brown (front-line) trenches. Also our shells falling in front of Gommecourt Wood; as we passed up Southern Avenue a shell burst

[12] So-called because of the black smoke they emitted on impact (after Jack Johnson, the Negro boxer).

close at our side and a piece fell between me and the stretcher-bearer behind me.

[*Wednesday, 3rd January*]

At Flag Avenue. Found that Fritz had battered the trench in four places during the night. His observation posts can see the new earth thrown up on top of the trench walls. Probably the reason why he does not drive us out by day is that he has working parties of his own busy on a new trench and heavy shelling of us would at once provoke retaliation. A fairly quiet day until about 1 p.m. A light rain falling.

[*Thursday, 4th January*]

Steady, soaking rain all the morning and trenches filled up again with water. When we first began we found Flag Avenue knee deep in mud and water. In a day or two the water has been pumped out, the mud withdrawn with scoops, the sides battered off and revetted with expanded metal and angle irons, driven firmly in, wooden transoms with wedge-shaped ends driven firmly between the angle irons across the bottom of the trench; on these the trench boards are laid and where necessary nailed on a bridge of wooden pickets with a transom nailed across.

Worked on steadily in soaking rain. My waterproof waistcoat and waders kept me dry. Not many German shells came our way to-day. Only a few stray pieces found their way into the trench.

[*Friday, 5th January*]

A fine calm morning. Daylight came as we marched through Colincamps and already two of our aeroplanes were up aloft. Soon there were seven flying round and our artillery began to open up. Observation balloons were above the heavy guns in the rear and it was a pleasure to see our aircraft examining the new trench dug by the Germans whose artillery was reduced to silence almost all the morning. Once a Taube came over and was hotly received by our anti-aircraft fire. It quickly turned tail. Afterwards there were five Taubes in the air at once, but they kept well behind their own lines.

Meanwhile our artillery was heavily bombarding a German trench no more than 150 yards to the right of us, and spent bits of the British shells were falling in our trench. Huge spouts of earth were thrown into the air and descended in ever widening circles, splashing up the earth in powdery spurts just like a rainstorm on a pond of water.

All the morning this continued with no German reply. We were able

38

to stand looking over the top of the trench watching a wonderful sight. Only about 1 p.m. Fritz began to throw shells over Southern Avenue trench and Euston Dump as we were heading home. We were told that the British had lost No. 4 Bombing Post in the night as a preliminary to retaking it the following night, which was done.

[Saturday, 6th January]

Our last day in Flag Avenue trench. Again quiet with the British artillery very busy and Fritz silent in our direction but sending many shells over the new batteries halfway between Colincamps and Euston Dump. A clear morning and so we were unable to finish the traverse on which we were working. This was done by a night party from another platoon who were able to work on the top of the trench. Several whiz-bangs passed over us with their peculiar sullenness as we went homewards up Sackville Street trench, and buried themselves in the open about 100 yards behind us. The first comer of these shells is always disconcerting on account of the velocity and absence of warning of their approach. The previous night the shells pitched in Euston Dump and knocked out three of the RWF[13] and wounded four others. Our No. 12 Platoon was on the spot at the time. My mother's birthday.

[Sunday, 7th January]

A day of rest and clearing up before moving out of the line for 'rest' period.

Went to church service at 10.45 but found that none was being held – on the only Sunday when I was free from duty. Probably the Chaplain was on the move with the division.

[Monday, 8th January]

An early move. Reveille at 4.30, breakfast at 5, and all blankets were rolled by 7 a.m. and everything ready for transport. The column was to march to bus, falling in at 1 p.m.

We shall not be sorry to quit Courcelles, where our quarters at first were very damp and uncomfortable, latterly greatly improved by the provision of three tier beds made of chicken wire and canvas stretched over a wooden frame and put together by the Battalion carpenters.

Pouring rain with a high wind all night is succeeded by a bright morning, with naturally much liquid mud. After much packing up, clearing up, inspection of billets, we fall in punctually at 1 p.m. and

[13] Royal Welsh Fusiliers.

march off through Bertraincourt to Bus, only five or six kilometres. There we are to mount motor lorries by 2 p.m. We stand about until 4 p.m. in much mud, and then fall in and stand with full pack until 5 p.m. when the column of about 50 motor lorries rolls along. We mount then, from 20 to 28 men in each. I secure a seat in front with the driver. The lorries are geared low, their top speed is but 12 miles an hour, roads in places are bad and in all parts muddy and our average speed with the many halts is not more than a walking pace.

We move off – back through Bertraincourt on the Doullens road. Hour succeeds hour, rain comes on and then driving sleet and snow. We skirt Doullens and mount the bare hills towards Beauval, and run through several storms of bitter, stinging sleet, and are chilled to the bone.

At length we draw up in a comely French village, which proves to be Montrelet. The billet provided for our forty men is a barn, mud-built and rat infested as usual, and with mud floor. All the bench beds had been taken when I arrived. One I found out in the snow. It is carried in, but foolishly we did not sweep the snow from the top and soon it thaws and runs through in streams to the middle storey which I occupy. Sayers, a stretcher-bearer, kindly lends me an extra waterproof sheet. I remove boots and puttees, put on an overcoat, wrap a blanket round my feet and with rubber sheets beneath and rubber sheet above soon drop off to sleep soundly and forget the open door at my head and the water dripping from above.

[*Tuesday, 9th January*]

Awake at 7.30 to hear a cock crow! The first for months! Then the sound of church bells! And a small boy speaking in lively tones! We are back among civilisation once more.

Soon I got up, collected some water from the dripping roof, shaved and washed – after a fashion. Breakfast, and we are ready for the road again. One remark of the motor driver of the night before impressed itself on me. He said he had moved three lots of men into the line and three lots out in the last three days. All the men going in were very quiet. All the men coming out were worn and ill, but every party was singing! 'How quiet the guns are this morning' was a first remark by one of the men, and that explains much.

We fell in at 11 a.m. and marched off four kilometres to Candas. The cleanliness (comparative) of Mourcelet, nicely coloured fronts to the houses, blinds, curtains and even flowers in the windows, children running in the street, all show to our delight that we have left the firing line behind us, with its shrapnel shattered houses and scenes of desolation.

We march off with firm and even step and soon find our way to our quarters in Candas. For the men the quarters are the usual barns, with fairly rain-tight roofs, and marred mainly by a stinking pond in the yard. For the sergeants there is a dry if draughty stable fitted with chicken wire beds. When the platoon have reached their quarters, I go off with Sgts Spain and Fitch and have a fine meal in the sitting room of a cleanly French house.

When we enter Monsieur is sitting in the corner by the circular stove on which Madame is busily cooking. Little two-year-old Jeanne, flaxen-haired and with blue eyes, is running round the room. We order poached eggs with potato chips, bread and butter and cafe au lait, and realise that it is the first egg we have seen for seven weeks! Before we leave the house Monsieur has gone into the next room and is weaving canvas on a hand loom. We enjoy a civilised meal once more sitting on a four-legged chair.

At 6 p.m. No. 9 Platoon is ordered to fall in and march to the railway station for fatigue duties. The boys have to come away without their tea, but march off in the best of spirits, singing gaily. Though the promised rest means but a chance of work, the relief from the strain of shell-fire is evident in the buoyant feelings of all. At Courcelles no one gave a thought to the matter and yet the banging night and day of our heavy guns near at hand, the occasional bombardments by Fritz, and the daily or nightly risks when 'up the line' make up a slight but steady strain which one only realises when the origin of it is removed.

At the railway station we are to unload timber trucks, and wait on a chilly evening more than two hours for the arrival of the train. At length the officer puts us to move heavy bulks of timber – merely to pass the time.

When the train comes in there are thirty trucks to be emptied. The load is one of heavy baulks of timber, used probably for gun pits and emplacements. The work goes on well tackled by some, whilst others are physically incapable of carrying out the heavy work. At length all the trucks are emptied, but it is well nigh midnight before we get back to quarters.

[Wednesday, 10th January]

We wake to cockcrow in our new quarters. Reveille is at 7 a.m. and the usual army breakfast of bacon and tea is very welcome. I look forward to a day of rest, with perhaps an unloading job in the evening. But about 10 a.m. I am given the job of Company Orderly Sergeant and take over my duties at once. The four platoons are billeted in five of the usual French barns, not so very far apart, but with the inevitable dunghill approach. After dark one requires all one's senses to steer safely round each of the backyards. And one of my principal duties is to call the men at reveille!

I attend at the Orderly Room at 9.12 and 6.30 and take sundry messages between the CO and the officers' billets. My limited French vocabulary proves itself a great help in finding my way about, and I am even regarded as somewhat of an oracle by my fellow sergeants whose wants I endeavour to voice.

The weather is cold and showery with occasional falls of snow that happily thaws. The frosts set a layer of ice on the ponds and our washing water.

[*Thursday, Friday and Saturday, 11th, 12th and 13th January*]
My formal duties as Orderly Sergeant continue, and there is little to record. Coal is now obtainable at the railway station, and we no longer shiver in our billets.

[*Sunday, 14th January*]
Church bells at 5.30 a.m. Up at 6.30 and find the ground covered with snow and the trees showing in feathery outline against a dark sky. The village street, with the ice-covered pond, the snow-clad houses and church in the background, make up a typical Christmas card scene.

On Saturday I witnessed one quaint and primitive sight. An old man of some eighty summers shuffles along down the street, bravely beating a roll on his weather-worn drum. He is the official town-crier, and his message is given in a highpitched and quavering voice.

Each day several British battalions march through and most have their bands at the head.

[*Monday, Tuesday and Wednesday, 15th, 16th and 17th January*]
On Thursday our only duties were the unloading of 21 trucks of hut parts. Have a bath! This consists of a sprinkle falling from a pipe laid across the ceiling, providing a trickle of fairly warm water, and this comes to us as a great luxury, and I am so far the only one to arrange it.

A good mail for me in the evening with a letter from Maud, Col Williams, J.C. Woods and a parcel from home.

On Friday 'standing by' all day but no train arrived at the station for unloading. Buy a French daily paper and converse with the family where my washing is done, and also at the house where I get coffee. I learn that at the beginning of the war German patrols rode through Candas, Lens, Amiens and Doullens. At Candas they raised some money at the point of the revolver. Most of the people fled as refugees. They do not like to talk of it and ask me why I want to know. I reply it is 'pour information pour moi et pour m'amuser!' Then they are satisfied.

[*Saturday, 20th January*]

Some sayings by Sgt Dyke: 'I love ferrets. I love a ferret better than a wife.' 'I never sneaks anything except from where it can be spared. I am like Robin Hood and if he had been alive today I should have mucked in with him.'

Was ordered to appear before the Colonel. After a few questions was handed over to the Adjutant and received a paper to fill in. Sgt Williams was with me at the Depot, at Blyth (as my CSM), at Sheerness, Le Havre, and at Courcelles and Candas, was before the Colonel at the same time. On comparing notes I found he was born on Feb. 27th, 1897 – one day later than I.

Weather continues cold and frosty with snow laying on the ground and roofs. 'Madcaps' gave concert in which Adjutant Fumall took part.

[*Sunday, 21st January*]

Due to appear before the MO.[14] Waited two hours only to learn that MO was ill and in bed. Again cold and frosty. Spent rest of day in writing and reading.

[*Monday, 22nd January*]

Warned to appear before MO but learned that he was again in bed. Warned to visit MO in afternoon and found him in bed. Was asked a few formal questions and was passed as fit – at a few paces distance, the doctor filling in the paper with an indelible pencil. Returned to Orderly Room where the Adjutant warned me not to go in for machine-gun work!

[*Tuesday, 23rd January*]

Woke up cold about 6 a.m. Found that water in a basin indoors was coated with ice! Yet we had two good fires going when we went to bed. A very hard frost and bitter wind blowing. Went out at 8.30 in charge of half platoon. Our work was at Ammunition Store about ½ mile from village, adjoining the railway. There a number more German prisoners were putting up sheds, whilst our men were building sandbag walls

---

[14] Medical Officer.

about 7 feet thick, carried right up to the roof, and separating the sheds for high explosive into many compartments. Walking about and supervising the work was bitterly cold.

A good mail from home on returning. We reached our billets at 4.30 p.m. Read and wrote for remainder of evening.

[*Wednesday, 24th January*]

Again very cold and sponge inside spongebag was frozen stiff.

Again out with working party on ammunition dump, returning at 4.30.

[*Thursday, 25th January*]

Cold continues but a bright sunny morning and dazzling light on the snow which lies six inches deep all over the fields in the open country.

Fell in at 8.05 a.m. and marched off in charge of No. 9 to Rosel, 4½ miles over a hard high road. Our work was to cut a trench by the side of the railway, for drainage purposes. As we were telling off the men for the task, P.C. Phipps, one of the twin brothers of No. 9, was just ahead of me and suddenly disappeared through some ice up to his armpits in water! He was quickly taken out and taken to an RE hut to dry himself by a small fire.

Rosel is a railway siding used for a huge provision and oil dump. About mid-day a fire broke out in a canvas tent which blazed freely. Three or four Minimax extinguishers were tried with some success but the fire burned for two hours or more. Fortunately the wind was blowing away from the oil stores.

Returned home in open trucks about 3.15 p.m. Fetched my usual ration of milk for supper cocoa and had a long conversation with the women of 73 and 45, both old women who carry on the farm.

[*Friday, 26th January*]

Again marched to Rosel on work of drainage. A biting cold wind and not much sun. Limber with mid-day ration failed to arrive and we had none of the bread and cheese and hot tea. No train to-day so we marched home. Sgt Wilson went to interview the GOC[15] re commission.

---

[15] General Officer in Command.

[Saturday, 27th January]

A day of duty with an inspection parade in the morning. In the afternoon 9 and 10 platoons played 11 and 12 at football. A good game with No. 9 as the better team ended in a draw 1–1, thanks to the machinations of the referee (Sgt Thistleton) and to Corporal Mainwaring in goal for No. 11.

At night got word of an early move in the morning. Two men at the station waiting to go on leave lay down for a rest and were frozen stiff and dead.

[Sunday, 28th January]

Reveille at 6. Still keen frost. A hasty move. Blankets to be rolled, equipment put together, much dumping of extra kit which the valise with much straining will not hold. Fall in at 8.30 and move off at 9 a.m. for Sartou via Doullens and Orville.

A keen wind and bright sun shining on the fields of snow. Roads in places very slippery and there were several falls. The Adjutant as he passes me said: 'You are for Blighty on the 3rd. What do you think of it?' I do not attach much importance to this. It seems too good to be true!

We march on steadily and cover the 10 miles by 12.30 p.m. For the night we settle down in Bow Huts, and soon have a fire burning in the little stove. After a meal of tinned salmon, which I brought with me, and army biscuits, I am still hungry. With Laidlaw and Thistleton I go to Sartou to have the eggs, bread and coffee which all our men favour. Also Tangerine oranges (at 2d each) – the first oranges this winter – which are really good.

To bed early with a change of socks – a rare event – and application of grease, for the half-inch soles on my boots are rather trying.

[Monday, 29th January]

Reveille at 7 a.m. Awake at intervals in the night, for it is almost too cold to sleep. In the morning our boots are frozen as stiff as a board and the water in our bottles is solid. Breakfast, and we clean up the huts, and are ready to move off.

Away we go towards Ransart, retracing our steps via Orville and the outskirts of Doullens. Several long halts, as the transport ahead of us has become blocked. On and through the streets of Doullens, familiar to me as the spot where I was left behind as my first travelling duty. We mount slowly a steep hill, and our backs are sorely tried by our loads. With the souvenirs I am carrying my pack weighs probably 60lbs. At the top of the hill 3 kilometres out, we find our billets in the village of Haute Visee. We sergeants are in a huge brick barn with thick brick walls, and straw on the floor, but no door, with the thermometer many degrees below freezing point. Owing to the straw no fire is possible.

As soon as the platoon has had its dinner sent up, I go off merrily with Sgts Laidlaw and Dyke and Thistleton down to Doullens for a meal. A friendly eating-house and six fried eggs, plenty of bread and butter and coffee stay our hunger. In part only, for as soon as we find the street, we decide upon some tea. An apricot tart, round and open, is cut into four and we have some dish water tea to go with it.

A motor lorry carries us 'home'. In Orders (Battalion) that night I am notified to report myself to Orderly Room at 6 p.m. on Feb. 2nd with a view to proceeding to a Cadet School in England. It does not seem a reality that I am to go to Blighty, and with the uncertainties of the Army and the impossibility of getting a letter off I decide not to write home. A good bed on the straw but a cold night.

[*Tuesday, 30th January*]

We march off through slight squalls of snow with a bitter wind in our teeth. We make for Frevent and passing through that place have a picnic lunch of pork and beans stew, seated in the snow by the wayside.

Quite a number of men have fallen out today for the roads are snow coated and then frozen so that the work of marching is almost doubled. On we go to our destination at Oeufs-en-Ternois (a 17 mile march).

Our billet is again a barn with plenty of straw, and I have the best bed since leaving Blighty. An enquiry off an old woman leads me to a farmhouse, where I have a fine meal of eggs, pate – a home-made brawn, and the usual cafe au lait, but made mostly of milk. Afterwards seven or eight fellow sergeants visit the same place, and we breakfast there the next morning.

[*Wednesday, 31st January*]

An early start with a heavy march before us. We travel via Pol to Baillou-beau-Corneille, only to find that the cavalry have forestalled us and we have to face another 5 kilometres (making 15 miles on slippery roads). Magnicourt is our destination. Supper in a homely farmhouse, a very damp billet. After supper visited another farmhouse, sat by the fireside and drank bowls of new milk. Sgt King was with me and his carbuncle excited keen sympathy.

[*Thursday, 1st February*]

On our journey once more, and reach Ambrines. We have been moving almost in a circle round St Pol and Frevent, and crow flight progress has been but small. A fair billet in a very drafty barn. A truss of hay from the loft made me a fine bed. Lame through twisting left ankle.

[*Friday, 2nd February*]

A day's rest. Receive orders to proceed to Penin, a village a few miles away, to appear before GOC. Go down at 3 p.m. on post cart. Interview at 5.50 and I spend the time in a warm cafe. A few questions from the General and a wait of an hour for the Staff Captain who told me I was due for Blighty on File 5, 6 or 7. Walked back painfully to Ambrines. Saw Adjutant who arranged for me to ride in blanket motor lorry in the morning.

[*Saturday, 3rd February*]

Left on motor lorry for Arras at 11 a.m. Spent four hours at Givenchy, for no one enters Arras until after dusk. Visited church and parts of town. At dusk we rose into Arras and find a guide awaiting us at the city gates. Signs of shell fire and bombs are visible. (The parts most affected are the gates, railway station and Cathedral with neighbouring Museum).

We halt in a fine street to unload blankets, and as we do so several shells whistle over our heavy guns in the rear. Some 18-pounders in a neighbouring street open up, and the explosions echo loudly in the empty streets. We soon learn that no one walks the streets in daylight because of aircraft.

Our own billet is a fine house in a side street. Opposite is a row of houses smashed by shell-fire – some are a mere heap of stones. We settle down in a lofty room – probably the morning room – with two large windows and every pane of glass is missing. It is freezing hard even with a small fire burning, and we spent the coldest night for some time.

[*Sunday, 4th February*]

Parade at 11.30 and march off through the Market Square, past a battered church of fine proportions, to the outskirts of the town. Street barricades are in evidence and when we halt behind the last of these we are within 300yds of our front line. All is very quiet, except for occasional trench mortars.

Our task is to dig a communication trench and the work lasts until 5 p.m. All Quiet. In the evening we go out by moonlight. We find a splendid Museum with one wing a mass of piled stones. Nearby is the Cathedral. A splendid towering pile but the roof shattered and fallen with the exception of a single arch, where nave joins choir, and broken masonry piled 20ft high in the nave. There was a pathway fairly clear up the aisles, the roof of which had not fallen. A shell-hole right through the pavement revealed the brazier fire of some British infantry billeted in the crypt (the Middlesex Regt I believe). Pencil cannot describe the towering masses of crumbling masonry outlined in the moonlight. No more evidence could be found of proof of wanton ruthlessness and vengeful spoliation.

[Monday, 5th February]

A day of formal parades. We are off to the trenches at 5.30 and find ourselves digging a communication trench near our front lines. The work is set out in front of some fine buildings through which the trench has to be dug. As we come through the building Fritz opens up with a machine gun in our front. All crouch close to the ground and as the gunner makes his traverse we hear the bullets whistle past. None or few strike the building and we realise that he is firing at the front line, and the bullets are going high over us. A second and a third time he opens fire within two or three minutes and we think we are 'spotted'. All is quiet again and we settle down to work.

The trench winds snake-like through a road made up of granite setts, and hard work by one of our best men allows him to raise one stone only as a result of hours' work! At 10.30 the relieving party arrives and we return home, in brilliant moonlight and keen frost. We go through the railway station, the scene of stiff fighting in 1914.

[Tuesday, 6th February]

Leave for Blighty!

2
September 1917 to January 1918: The Ypres Salient

Left home at 5 o'clock. A brave farewell from wife and daughter. Son and baby scarcely know what the parting means.

Off by the 5.26 train and an easy run to Waterloo. As I stepped out of the carriage and was seeking my kit, shouts of 'Take cover! Take cover!' echoed hoarsely round the station. Some at once ran for cover, others moved more slowly, but the lowering of the lights hastened their decision. Without my kit I took refuge in the City Tube and waited patiently, as the inner passages of the Tube filled with families from a poor neighbourhood, many of them foreign Jews with crowds of scared children. Soon the anti-aircraft guns opened up, fairly freely, and at times falling shrapnel brought down tinkling glass from the station roof. A few dull thuds denoted the dropping of enemy bombs. For two hours we waited, the guns bursting out afresh each time we were about to move.[1]

At last I found my kit in a heap on the platform and slowly dragged my valise to the North London Tube. Here with the help of a friendly policeman I made my way to the lift and thence through more crowds of sleepy children to the train. At Oxford Circus two boys about 3ft nothing high seize my valise and drag it between them with insistent shouts of 'Gangway, please!' 'Clear the gangway!'

Thence without incident to Holland Park where a kindly welcome awaits me. Supper, a short talk, and in the words of Pepys of old – so to bed!

[*Monday, 1st October*]

Awake at 5.45. Quickly dress and leave for Victoria. A thick fog envelopes us, though there is promise of sunshine later. Reach Victoria at

---

[1] During the week ending 2nd October, 97 German bombers ('Gothas') attacked London with 448 bombs. Thousands of the poorer residents of the city moved into the Underground stations, ignoring attempts by staff to stop them (H.G. Castle, *Fire Over England*, Leo Cooper 1982). The scars from these attacks can be clearly seen on the base of Cleopatra's Needle on the Embankment.

7.15 and find the waiting train already full. Secure a seat in a Pullman car and find many friends and acquaintances assembled on the platform and amongst them Everest and Gayton of the Dorsets. Soon Jim Hart arrives and I have a good send-off.

Uneventful journey to Folkestone, which we reach about 9.45. We report by regiments to the RTO[2] and are then free until 1 p.m. With Everest and Gayton I make my way to the Leas, we receive the wishes of 'Good Luck' of several inhabitants. A visit to the Post Office to send off home letters, and then a call upon Temple, from whom a friendly greeting and 20 minutes chat. Luncheon (at an outrageous price!) at a restaurant, and then down to the boat, the 'Princess Clementine' of Ostend, a fast paddle steamer, not a big cargo boat such as the 'Archimedes' by which I crossed on my last 'trip'.

A comfortable seat on the upper deck, life-belts are donned, and we sit basking in the sun waiting for the boat to leave the quay. There are three crowded ships and the slowest is the first to leave. Ours follows and one of the fast turbine cross-Channel boats brings up the rear. We are escorted by three torpedo boats, in front and on the flanks, and a fast airship follows after us keeping watch and ward against lurking submarines. There is scarcely a movement on the sea, and quickly the cliffs grow dimmer. Ere we are halfway across 'Old Blighty' has faded away in a wall of mist.

In 1¾ hours we are outside the harbour, and it is some time before we get to our moorings. Then there are the usual reports to be made and the sorting of baggage, all amid the strangely familiar setting of a French quayside. It is well nigh dark as we (16 officers all told) rumble out of the Docks in a motor lorry and climb the steep hillside to the camp of Osterhove. We had crossed, 15 Dorsets together, and on landing receive our orders to be divided between the RB[3] and KRRC. Everest and Gayton are for the RB and with amazement and some delight I am ordered to join the Rifles yet again! So it is the 'Army unexpected' that has happened once again.

Once on top of the hill at Osterhove we are told off five in a tent and have our first experience of sleeping in a valise. It is a brilliant moonlight night, the searchlights are busy, and not without cause. For tonight it is the turn of Boulogne to be bombed by many aircraft. The Archies are busy in reply and vigorous salvos of light shrapnel burst overhead. Then firing dies away, twice to be renewed as the enemy circle overhead yet again.

[2] Railway Transport Officer.
[3] Rifle Brigade.

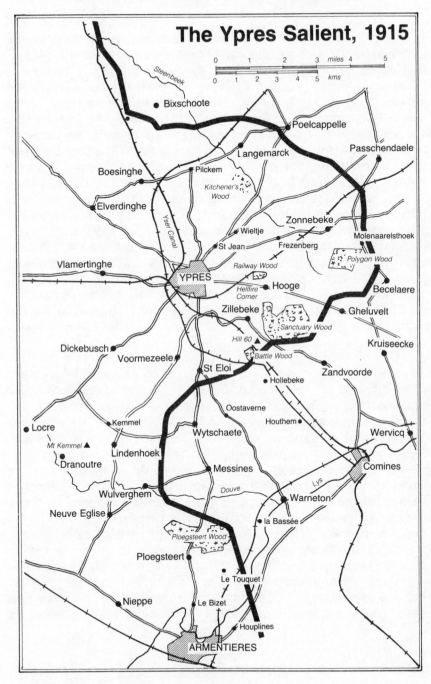

The Ypres Salient, 1915

[*Tuesday, 2nd October*]

It is a fine morning when we woke to the humorous greeting of the Quartermaster Sgt with a genial call of 'Show a leg, gentlemen, please!'

At 8.30 we move off quickly down the hill to the station and spend an hour at the little Officers' Club ere the train is due to leave. We travel comfortably, four in a compartment and can smile at the thoughts of 42 to a horse truck, as in former times. It was fortunate that we have laid in some store of food from a canteen, as for 14 hours we jog along at trooptrain speed without a chance of buying food. The men have had their issue of rations, but small wonder is it that two trucks of apples at Aumale cause them to fill their hats and pockets, even shirts and handkerchiefs, with stores of cider windfalls. Of the after-effects of this indulgence I have no record. But a gang of German prisoners down the line were greeted with a withering fire of well aimed apple cores.

Our track lies through a fertile river valley. Old men and women and German prisoners are gathering the second or maybe third crops of water meadow hay. On each side there are orchards of cider apples, hanging in scarlet or russet ropes, small fruit but of glorious hues. In truth it is the fairest stretch of French soil I have crossed, at least in my army wanderings.

[*Wednesday, 3rd October*]

All had dropped off to sleep and awoke to shouts of 'Harfleur', our destination, and we find that the fair weather of the day has given way to pouring rain. A guide awaits us – it is 1.30 a.m. – and we make our way to the familiar camps on the hillside, and only report our presence.

Delay, and finally we pass on to No. 16 Camp. In the Mess ante-room we receive three blankets apiece and settle down to a good, if short, sleep on the floor. At 8 a.m. we appear before the Colonel, a gentleman of the old Army type. Thence we make our way to No. 9 Camp and are parted from our Rifle Brigade friends.

Light duties today – merely drawing gas helmet and box respirator, and journey up to the Pimple, where we pass through the testing chambers. Then quickly down the hill and away to Le Havre where we have tea and dinner at the useful Officers' Club. Back by 9.30 and early to bed – a valise spread out on two or three empty packing cases – in a square canvas hut with a corrugated iron roof, a dwelling house for two.

[*Thursday, 4th October*]

Heavy rain in the night. A light day's work on the Pimple, merely anti-gas drill and lectures in the morning. After lunch down to the Ordnance

52

stores in Havre to draw some trench boots and other extras. Dinner and a good bath at the Officers' Club, and back at 9.30 to receive orders to act as Conducting Officer of a draft of 55 men to our destination.

[*Friday, 5th October*]

Report at 9 a.m. to the Adjutant of No. 16 Camp and receive my orders, which I read to the assembled draft. An inspection by the CO and off we march by muddy roads to Le Havre entraining sheds, now a familiar spot. Rations are drawn, a picquet of 40 of our men is set, and we wait for the train to be made up – five hours of army patience.

Soon after 4 p.m. we are away on a train some 600 to 800 yards long. Slowly we move but steadily, with few of the exasperating halts of a year ago. There are five of us in a 1st class compartment, and this is comfortable indeed compared with 42 in a horse truck! A halt and hot tea about 8.30 p.m. at Busch(?). Livened by this, we talk together until 11.30 p.m. and then settle down for the night. Earlier in the evening we had played solo whist by the light of a candle on a window ledge. Our issue of rations is the usual 'Bully', jam, and cheese, and teeth-testing biscuits, and this we supplement by chocolate, French bread and apples.

[*Saturday, 6th October*]

Sleep fairly well but fitfully, and wake about 7 a.m. to find ourselves approaching Boulogne! We dress quickly in hopes of a good breakfast, but this is not to be. Our train skirts the town, follows the coast, and heads for Calais. This we leave on our left and we pass on to the NW and away to Hazebruck, first passing St Omer where only the tower of the fine abbey was to be seen from the train. At Hazebruck we have time for a wash and a meal ere we go on to Bailleul. There we detrain and I am glad to find the men of my draft complete, rations and all. My fellow officer, Martin, also has charge of a draft and is unlucky enough to have had two men left behind on the way.

We march off about 7 kilometres to our camp, in a swampy field, and report after dark. We get dinner and make the best of the situation sleeping on our valises on the wet ground. It is no great hardship for we get hold of sufficient blankets.

[*Sunday, 7th October*]

A pouring wet morning. No duty for us until noon, when we turn out for a muster parade of the whole camp for the purpose of rearranging tents. This lasts for an hour in drenching rain. Lunch, and then Martin and I receive orders at 2.20 to be packed and ready to march off to our Battalion at 3 p.m. We leave about 3.30 and make our way by road towards Birr Barracks, Locre.

Just outside the camp we meet Green, ex-Sgt of 24th KRR, now an officer of Royal Warwicks Labour Battalion. He told us of a short cut by a muddy track, over Mont Noir to Locre. This we follow in a downpour of rain. There is a high wind blowing, and as we reach the top of the hill there is a break in the clouds, and we step over the frontier into Belgium pondering for a moment what that war-ridden country may have in store for us. The sun breaks through the clouds and we can see far away over the Belgium plain, with the flash of guns in a curving line away in front of us.

A signpost has shown us 9 kilos to Ypres (Yper) as its dual rendering is thereon shown. Down the hill and we steer for the square-towered church of Locre and on to the KRR camp. We report ourselves, are made at home in the Mess, and I am allotted to 'A' Company, Martin to 'C' Company. 'A' Company and Headquarters mess together. We are quartered in comfortable huts, and learn that the Battalion is resting, and expecting to be sent back to the 'line' at any time.

[*Monday, 8th October*]

Next morning we go onto the range at 7 a.m., and drill on the parade ground etc., follows. In the afternoon a brief route march for the Battalion. 'Cuckoos' concert in evening.

[*Tuesday, 9th October*]

Routine duties with Company route march in the afternoon. McCulloch, Park and Johnson, three Dorset officers from Weymouth, rejoin us in the evening. I am lucky to have McCulloch as my companion in 'A' Company. His valise has gone astray and he has to settle down in some discomfort for the night.

[*Wednesday, 10th October*]

A wet morning, and gas drill, etc. in the huts. Brief route march in the afternoon. 'Barn Owls' concert in evening, a fine Divisional company.

[*Thursday, 11th October*]

Another day of training with route march round by Dranontre. To bed early in evening.

54

[*Friday, 12th October*]

Company training and short route march up Kemmel Hill, whence can be seen eastern end of Ypres, and the smoke stacks of Lille away to the south. A hazy morning, in spite of which a fine view.

There are rumours that we are to move into the Salient on the morrow, and the view of 'the Promised Land' shows only a wide water-logged plain with blasted trees, overtopped by a wide arc of captive balloons. Gun flashes and shell-bursts break the view.

In the afternoon football 'sixes' for the Company – five minutes each way – very amusing. In the evening receive moving orders. I am to go up with the advance party to view the land.

[*Saturday, 13th October*]

Morning of preparations. We move off at 12.30 and for the first time enter the Ypres Salient. We are fairly lucky in catching motor lorries, but the weather is against us, and heavy rain squalls burst over us in succession. We go in by way of Ridge Wood, to Jackson's Dump, getting a lorry ride as far as 'the Brickstack'. Then we come into the shell-hole area, and the duckboard tracks are very faulty and broken by shell-fire.

We reach the famous Canadian(?) tunnels and thence make for Brigade Headquarters, now in pouring rain, and over ground not a yard of which has been unstirred by shell-fire. Not a living creature can exist there – even the rats are missing – only man, and mud! It is a wilderness and a solitary place, nothing whole remains. Littered around are the debris of broken rifles, soaked and torn equipment, twisted wire and stakes, with thick brown mud slowly but surely covering all.

There are no trenches to be seen, with orderly revetments, fire-step and duckboard tracks. This is a warfare of linked shell-holes, or detached posts and strong points; for the artillery dominates all set positions such as aeroplane photos can disclose.

At Brigade HQ the three other officers, who are in advance of the party, go down below for instructions. As we wait the Bosch shells come sufficiently near, so we take temporary shelter in the dug-out entrance. It is growing dark as we move on to the Battalion HQ of the Somersets, whom we are to relieve. There we find the CO and Adjutant, with gum boots, sitting in a dugout of which the floor is a foot under water. We get our instructions, and the offer of a drink of whisky, which at the first attempt is spoiled, for the orderly instead of water has poured in paraffin!

It is now dark as we move off and the rain is pouring down. I learn that half the company (my company) is to relieve in close support, so I move off with the others. We go cross-country, through the swamps, gradually dipping until we come to the Bassevillebeck, a morass which we wade knee deep in mud. Thence up and down several slopes as we scramble and slide along the slippery little ridge that divides the shell-hole lakelets. Most of the party stick firmly in the mud and have to be helped out. One or two fall head foremost into shell-holes and are dragged out slimy and dripping.

Now we are approaching our front-line post and move with caution. We are there, in pouring rain, and find a little platform dug into the side of the slope, just below the summit of the ridge – a couple of planks for a low seat and waterproof sheets rigged up overhead as a rough covering from the weather. At the far end crouches an officer with a shaded candle by him and on the planks are huddled a few men, waiting their turn of sentry duty. Over the ridge only 30 yards away are the Bosch posts, and their voices can be heard. Neither side can see the other even by day, but both parties are in view of the ridge – due west and 200 yards away from where the close supports lie. Thither, after a wait of perhaps half an hour, my small party makes its way.

I find myself in a concrete dugout on the top of a ridge, filled by four or five officers, and the floor under a foot of water which gives off a most unsavoury smell. We three KRR officers join the party, and settle down as best we can on the lower tiers of the plank beds ranged round the walls. We are wet almost to the thighs, our boots full of water, and it is not easy to sleep when one's feet are chilled. German machine-gun bullets patter at intervals on the walls, but there is no shelling, for the rival positions are too indefinite for artillery purposes. We sleep in snatches.

[Sunday, 14th October]

We wake to hear it is a fine morning, and bodies of both British and Hun can be plainly seen, showing where the attack was made a few days before. (The British reached their objective, but with too few men left to hold the position, and shelling and strong MG fire from a ridge on the right drove them back to their original line.) Several Huns are on the move, and one is seen surveying our position through his glasses, until a sniping shot from our doorway makes him lower his head.

All day we lie 'doggo' in the dugout, partly because of the machine gun trained on the door, and partly because no good was to be got by going outside. Late in the day we receive orders to return to our Battalion which after all is not to take over this part of the line.

At nightfall we recall our officer from the advanced post and move quickly out of the doorway, away through the shattered wood which lies to the south. We hurry our progress to the tune of machine-gun bullets, which are spelling 'Phut, Phut' in the mud somewhere short of us. We drop down the slope, cross the Bassevillebeck once more knee deep in slime, and push on up the further slope, through the slippery maze of shell-holes. It is a starry night, not too dark, and the stumps of trees have probably covered our movements. Soon we strike the duckboard track, and make swift progress along it. We have been dripping with sweat and thoroughly breathless by reason of our hasty rush through the morass.

A halt is called while two of our party go off to pick up two HQ men who have gone on to the nearest aid post. Meanwhile we find that three of the servants – mine included (for the second time!) – have been left behind in the scurry. They are old hands and we leave them to make the best of their way 'home' themselves – which they do the next morning.

We move on again at high speed, for shrapnel going overhead warns us to hurry. Away we go making for Jackson's Dump and on until at last we get a welcome lorry lift on our way, as far as Kemmel. A short tramp, another lorry, and we are back at Locre in a little over four hours from the time of leaving the front line! The news that awaits us is much as we expected. We are to move off on the morrow and take part in an attack, and it is practically in the same district as I had just visited.

[Monday, 15th October]
Wake from a good night's rest, and prepare to move off to take our place in the battle line in an attack. We march as far as Ridge Wood Camp where we settle down for the night, some of the men in tents and some in bivouacs. In the evening news comes through that the attack has been put off or given over to other troops. We can only feel much relieved, for our task would have been no easy one!

[Tuesday, Wednesday and Thursday, 16th, 17th and 18th October]
Three days spent in training. In the afternoon footer 'sixes' once more, every man of each platoon taking his share. On Wednesday we end up with a whole Company game, forty or more a side. I have never played in a bigger scrimmage and it was a wonder no one was hurt.

On Thursday there was a Brigade rugger match in which I was asked to take part, but someone else filled the gap. Our Brigade won easily by 26 points to nil.

[*Friday, 19th October*]

A quiet day preparatory to going into the line. We move off at 4.30 and march by platoons steadily to Jackson's Dump, thence to Canada Tunnels where our guides meet us. We follow the duckboard slowly but steadily, for there are many parties on the move. All goes well until the track finishes, except that the tins of water are not to be found. After we leave the duckboard track after crossing the Bassevillebeck, we mount the slopes through the woods.

As we, or those just ahead of us, come over the crest, we are spotted by the Bosch on the ridge opposite, some 200 yards away. It is a moonless night and the shattered trees help to hide us. As usual Fritz is sending up a succession of his (fine) Very lights, while we send up none. One of those probably shows the incautious movement of a close file of men. Immediately hot machine-gun fire is opened up on us, and all hastily tumble into watery or muddy shell-holes and flatten themselves as best way they can. By this means the showers of bullets spatter almost harmlessly in the mud around. More serious are the 'French' Mortar bombs which fall in the midst of the party and cover us with a shower of mud and stones.

Fritz is sending up half a dozen Very lights at a time and all is as bright as day. We can see the figures of men running along the opposite ridge. The firing dies down and I make my way to the HQ dugout. Meanwhile the guides take the lead with the men to their close support 'funk-holes' scooped out of the rising ground on the further side of the dip. The Sgt reports that two men are missing, probably killed. He said they were lying together in a shell-hole when a trench mortar bomb fell right on top of them. I hope he may have been mistaken.

I take over from the RS[4] officer and then visit our line of posts in the valley. Return to dugout and by this time it is –

[*Saturday, 20th October*]

Go through various forms of receipt-giving and taking from RS Rgts. My heavy pack and equipment cause some laughter, but the clothing, etc. I have brought will all be useful. Sat in chair for rest of night and slept for several hours. Spent all day in dugout. At nightfall visited my CO's posts. It is now certain that Robinson and Gibson were knocked out the previous night, and send in casualty report accordingly. Fritz is so close that one of his Very lights set fire to a rubber sheet close to where I was standing.

At nine o'clock or soon after, the runner and I again visit our six

---

[4] Royal Signals.

posts and I distribute the rum to the men according to official orders. Water is short, only 1½ tins for 31 men; more will be sent up tonight.

[*Sunday, 21st October*]

Woke after a fine sleep on the wet floor, but my mackintosh cape and trench coat make a fine bed. Another fine morning, and it is fortunate the weather overhead is favourable. Fritz has the 'wind up' on this front. Snipers and MGs[5] are active at night, and from midnight to dawn he is putting a barrage on to the valley behind our ridge where he imagines that troops might be assembling. Our artillery night and day give him no peace, and occasional practice barrage must set him thinking. His snipers are most persistent; from where I am sitting I can see a neat hole scooped in the concrete, where his bullets from a fixed rifle strike across the doorway. I wear my equipment and revolver day and night, and tin hat and box respirator are close at hand.

Last evening we had in our dugout a wounded man shot through the shoulder. He was old looking, nearing forty, and sat there quiet but complacent. It was odd to note his smiling satisfaction in the thought of getting home to Blighty – 'the soldier's Home sweet Home!'

At night I visit the posts again. Learn that Gibson was shot through the head by a MG bullet, and Robinson was hit by a TM[6] bomb whilst in a shell-hole. Soon after my return Capt Hankey came up with a ration party. I go down to send all available men away to Co. HQ for our day's rations. Only the LGs[7] remain. I spend two hours down in shell-holes while the men are away. Return for some supper, and then once more down to the posts to dish out rum to the men. At 2 a.m. turn in to sleep, on the top tier of bunks. Wakened at 6 a.m.

[*Monday, 22nd October*]

Wakened by a heavy British barrage which swells to drum fire. In defiance of this the Bosch plays his MG in tattoos on our concrete walls, and his TM pops across towards our front door. One or two shells of heavier calibre drop close to hand, and one strikes the corner of the dugout extinguishing the lights within and chipping more fragments from its solid walls. To sleep once more and wake to breakfast at 10 a.m. Then in merry mood we all sing 'The Old Fashioned Town'. This paves the way to the following parody – a joint effort:

[5] Machine Guns.
[6] Trench Mortar.
[7] Lewis Guns.

The Old Concrete Dugout

There's an old concrete on the Bassevillebeck
And it faces old Gheluvelt town!
Though the rates and the taxes are not much per week,
New tenants walk in with a frown!
Yet tho' ev'ry night to the front line we go
To see that the 'boys' are OK,
We are not very slow,
In returning you know,
To sleep in the dugout all day!

Altho' in the dugout of beds there are four,
Of officers there are umpteen,
It is out of the question to sleep on the floor,
Past tenants have left it unclean!
To settle the Bosch that repose in the slime –
They have lain there for many a week! –
We sprinkle it freely with chloride of lime,
That dugout on the Bassevillebeck!

Of that old dugout the walls are so stout –
Some three to four feet, less or more –
A nine-inch direct hit would scarce knock it out,
Yet a sniper sits watching the door!
So keep your head low,
As you pass to and fro,
When at dusk you may wander and ream,
If you value your share
Of those faces so fair,
Or there's someone will miss you at home!

So much for 'our song' which we proudly sing to each visitor in turn, and to the tune, of course, of 'The Old-fashioned Town'.

Another barrage in the afternoon and a rather wild reply from the Bosch. In spite of the song, I make a bed on the wet floor with a rubber sheet laid on some planks; anything is better than sitting cramped all day on a bench.

Fritz has some sportsmen in his ranks! A new machine-gunner is watching over our doorway, and signals his advent with a series of tuneful displays against the concrete walls of the dugout; he had a firm but delicate touch as he raps out the long or staccato phrases of his little tunes. My half-company go off as ration carriers and duly return and settle down for the night after the customary rum issue. After midnight comes a letter from OC 'A' Co. ordering practically all the men to go down once more for rations, carrying one day's food with them! That means another day in the line for all of us.

[*Tuesday, 23rd October*]
My instructions include a visit to a neighbouring post. The moon has gone down, and it is my job to find the correct spot. It is very dark and for two hours my runner and I wander to and fro searching every shell-hole. After trying all the back area we turn toward the front line, and going carefully are surprised to find ourselves past the front posts and on our way towards the Bosch. A friendly turn is done us by a Bosch Very light and we scramble into one of our front posts. All enquiries are fruitless and we return reluctantly to our dugout with our task unfinished. We had found a crater post with waterproof sheet covering and shovels lying near, but probably due to the relief which we now learn to have taken place, the post was empty.

Return too wet and cold about the feet to sleep, so set to work to rub my feet, and a dry pair of socks and an early breakfast send me to sleep comfortably on my planks with the foul smelling water lapping the edges of the boards! In the afternoon sleep once more. No tea, for water is not forthcoming. No wash or shave since last Friday, and my beard is beginning almost to take shape. In the evening pay two visits to my posts. Each time held up by heavy Bosch shell-fire, which fortunately misses the mark. This time successfully connect up our posts to our neighbour with a tape. Very dark after moonset.

[*Wednesday, 24th October*]
Return at 2 a.m. and settle down to sleep. Breakfast at 8.30; it is the day of our relief and there is no inclination to sleep longer. Rain during the night and our quarters for the men are in a deplorable state. In our dugout the water slowly rises. Sunshine comes to improve the outlook, but water dries up slowly in the many lakelets that pit the ground.

One little incident of last evening may be set down here. We (my runner and self) were returning from our long round in search of our neighbouring post. We felt pleased as we found ourselves within 50 yards of our dugout. Suddenly we heard three rifle shots, almost a small volley. I stopped my runner and said I heard a man call as in distress. 'He's hit me! He's hit me!' At once I knew I must turn back and give help. We stopped to listen and hearing no more sounds my guide said: 'I think, Sir, he said seventeen sixty'![8] And so it proved. When Martin,

[8] i.e. 17th Battalion of the 60th.

a fellow officer, came in he told us of his adventure. As he approached one of the posts he heard me challenge, but was greeted with a burst of rifle fire. The men in the post were out of the ASC[9] and in 'the line' for the first time. Fortunately, they fired with an ASC aim! I was mistaken in the words he used. But his tone of voice was of a man under fire.

The hours drag slowly towards dusk and our relief. All are packed and ready before dark, and sit somewhat silent, pondering. All plans have been made, we are only waiting. By 6.30 we have had tea and move out to our posts in the shell-holes. It is moonlight, but a light rain is falling and that is in our favour. The Bosch seems to know what is coming and has advanced his Very lights so that they fall well within our lines, almost as far back as our close supports.

We sit quietly talking huddled in a shell-hole. About 8 o'clock the voice of the guide is heard. I go out and find 90 men of the South Staffs, under a Sgt-Major ready to replace 15 men, all that are left of my half-company. (Six have gone as guides, two killed, and nine down with trench feet!) About 30 get into our shell-holes, the rest settle down in the pouring rain to dig themselves in. In front we can see 'C' Company's relief pouring in. By the time my party is out, 'C' Company are upon us in a stream, and I find it impossible to get hold of my men. So I give the word to 'push on'. Fritz has just spotted us, when suddenly a barrage is opened by our artillery right on his lines and his advanced machine guns are smothered. It is bright as day with the stream of Very lights which the Hun sends up. The strong wind blowing from the Bosch lines and the driving sleet are in our favour. On we go to the duck-board track through the marsh behind us. Away as fast as we can scramble as his artillery is beginning to open up and his 'HE'[10] is searching for that duck-board track. I have to report at Battalion HQ 'Relief complete.'

The Adjutant requires my runner as a guide for the S. Staffs runners, so back to the track with this party, and then on alone along the track of my party. Off I go at once for the track for the moment is fairly clear. So for perhaps a quarter of a mile. Then I come across a small knot of men bending over two stricken men. One has a piece of shrapnel through the foot, and the other is in a sad way with his foot blown off and other injuries. He is still conscious. I lend my shell dressing and go in search of stretcher-bearers, but feel very helpless myself for such a case. Stretcher-bearers come along and we push on, at length falling in with the second half of 'A' Company, who had been in Reserve. Then I learn that trouble had fallen on the party of guides I sent down

[9] Army Sluice Corps.
[10] High Explosive.

62

the night before. A shell burst among them and killed LC Repp and Davies and wounded several others, including Langton (that makes the ½ Co. casualties up to four killed and wounded; 1 trench feet; 8 chilled feet; out of a total of 34 men).

Push on past many bad feet cases to Shrapnel Corner, where the Company cookers stand and serve out hot soup. Then a wait of hours for the motor lorries. More delays on the road. Daylight breaks and it is 6.30 a.m. before we reach our camp at Fermoy.

[Thursday, 25th October][11]
To bed in a hut with a dry floor to lie on. Rest until 10.30. Wake to pouring rain and a swampy camp. Rest all day.

[Friday, 26th October]
During the night a Bosch aeroplane paid us a visit and dropped a bomb only 50 yards from our hut. Fortunately it fell in soft earth and a bank screening us no damage was done. So I was told, for I slept soundly as usual. Rest all day and scarcely move outside the door. Write many letters. Hot bath at the Locre Hospice!

[Saturday, 27th October]
Wake to a fine morning and sunshine. Again resting. The only event of the day was an inspection parade. In the morning was sent for by CO and told that I should take over the Company during a short interregnum. It is a strange war, when a month's service sees one in charge (even temporarily) of a Company.

[Sunday, 28th October]
Move up to Vierstraat Camp, a change for the worse with mud ankle deep. McCulloch is sent off to the Reinforcement Camp for a spell as an instructor.

One incident of our spell 'up the line' deserves to be recorded. The characters concerned were Vynall, private secretary to Sir Tatton Sykes, a bit of a wag, and Pulley, a man of 36, out in France for the first time, and with a reputation of being a bit 'windy'! Both belong to 'D' Company. After due preparation Vynall begins: 'I say, Pulley, 'D' Company has got to do a bit of a patrol tonight. You know there is to be a bit of

[11] The Second Battle of Passchendaele was launched on this day. This was the final offensive of the Third Battle of Ypres.

a push tomorrow, and HQ wish us to examine the Bosch wire along our front and see if it has been properly cut.' 'Yes,' said Pulley rather doubtfully, 'but who is to do it?' 'Why, you, of course,' said Vynall. 'At least, one of us has got to do it, and it's your turn as I have already done one patrol.' 'What along the whole of our front? That must be 300 yards,' said Pulley, looking glum. After a pause, he added: 'Well, I am a married man with two children.' 'And I have two children too, and it's your turn,' said Vynall. Said Pulley: 'Well I know nothing about it at all.' 'Then you will d..n soon learn!' retorted Vynall; relenting a little he added (producing a pack of cards), 'Let's cut for it. Ace to count high.' 'All right,' said Pulley, seeing a gleam of hope. They cut and Vynall stands with an ace in his hand! Pulley draws a three! 'Now you must go!' said Vynall, but could contain himself no longer and the whole party shook with laughter. It was all a 'plant' and Vynall had carefully arranged the four aces at the bottom of the pack! Pulley's confusion was excelled by his relief from anxiety. From that day he won the name of 'the Wire King'.

[*Monday, 29th October*]

Spent part of the afternoon in examining the country away to the N. of us. Just as when we were at Ridge Wood Camp, we are set at the foot of Messines Ridge. The huge mine craters crown the top of the hill. Through my glasses much is visible. Our old front line winds along at the foot of the slope, and the old difficulties of supply are painfully obvious. The support trenches near us are rapidly falling in, the shell-holes are green with grass, and some of the shattered trees have begun to sprout. Suddenly my thoughts are interrupted by machine-gun fire. I turn my glasses and see about a dozen Bosch aeroplanes appearing from behind a cumulus cloud, and swooping down towards us in arrowhead formation. In the centre is a huge battle plane, the largest I have ever seen with fully twice the wing span of other machines. There is a buzz from all corners of the horizon. Our machines come climbing singly to the attack. The Bosch turns tail ingloriously and creeps into a big cloud!

Part of my afternoon was spent taking our men to the baths, where all get a good change of clothes. Am now Mess President for the Company.

[*Tuesday, 30th October*]

Wake in the night with our tent nearly blowing away. Have to turn out to peg it down properly. Strafe my servant, Bundock, a slow fellow, and tell him I can look after myself better than he can look after me! This with good effect, for the tent is well secured when I return in the afternoon. Promise to play a game of rugger against the Rifle Brigade, and am not wholly sorry when pouring rain cancels the match. I have played rugby perhaps three times in the past 21 years.

Receive a welcome copy of 'The Happy Warrior' and other verses from John Russell and his wife. Cannot expect to live up to such a standard! 'Tis well perhaps to follow, even at a distance!

A wet afternoon, and am writing this sitting up in bed, on the floor of my tent. Scott, a new subaltern, shares the tent with me. Aird, another new sub, came in last night, and is taking over my platoon.

[*Wednesday, 31st October*]

In the morning the Colonel meets me and offers me the job of under-study to the Quartermaster! I reply that I am 'not keen on that branch of the work' and hope I do not appear ungrateful! Go to Adjutant and suggest Pulley for the job. Suggestion adopted and Pulley enthusiastically grateful!

[*Thursday, 1st November*]

To bed early, expecting to move up the line on following day. Wake in night with a rocking of tent and quaking of earth. Turn over instinctively and promptly, expecting the shower of debris which follows an explosion. A few seconds and showers of mud and small stones fall on the tent sides and harmlessly off. Turn over and to sleep again! Daylight shows that an aeroplane bomb has fallen in a line with and forty yards from our tent. Its force was expended in a slight trench in which it fell, but the crater shows itself ten yards across, ten feet deep, and now filling with water!

Boney, second in command of Company, has now gone to signalling school, and I go to share Capt Hankey's tent. In evening learn that orders for up the line are cancelled. In bed at 10.35 p.m. Receive Orderly Room note that I have been 'selected to attend Special Course of Instruction at 2nd Army School'. A three to five weeks course! Am not wholly pleased, as am getting interested in work of Company.

[*Friday, 2nd November*]

An uneventful day. In evening 41 of our Company told off for working party under REs at Australia Tunnel.

[*Saturday, 3rd November*]

On parade with remnant of about 18 men. A dull misty day with low clouds. Suddenly a Fritz plane darts from the clouds and flies in swift zigzags or curves, like a snipe, right over our camp. Shrapnel bursts in front and behind, Lewis guns and rifles take up the tune, but he disappears in the clouds behind us. A half an hour, and three aeroplanes are seen darting and twisting over our lines. Lewis guns open fire, riflemen seize their rifles and open with 'rapid'. Twisting and turning in a hail of hasty fire they pass behind us, leaving us wondering if after all they were our machines, or as we supposed captured Britishers flown by daring Fritzers, but under the guise of British colours.

[*Sunday, 4th November*]

Still remaining at Vierstraat No. 1 Camp until –

[*Wednesday, 7th November*]

When we move about half a mile to Dead Man's Farm, no change for the better except that we officers occupy splendid dugouts, the strongest and driest that I have yet entered. The previous night very heavily bombed by Fritz aeroplanes. None came near us but dozens of bombs were unloaded on the camps around, and our canvas head cover seemed very inadequate as we lay and listened.

[*Thursday, 8th November*]

Wet again. Move off to Balleul and spent night there at Rue des Poissons. Comfortable enough in a typical French room which I shared with Thomas of the Rifle Brigade. To propitiate the English guests a print of the 'Farewell to Nelson' adorns the walls.

[*Sunday, 11th November*][12]

Rose at 6 a.m. and caught 8.08 train to St Amer, a quiet old place. Lunched at Hotel du Commerce where Winston Churchill[13] was at a table opposite me! Found our way on foot to the old Convent(?) where the second Army Central School is situated. A hugh rambling chilly building.

Here for five weeks I went through a general course of instruction.

[12] The Third Battle of Ypres is officially declared 'ended' on this day. It would be more accurate to say that the offensive had finally foundered.
[13] Churchill was the Minister of Munitions. On 18th November he attended a conference in Paris with his French and Italian opposite numbers.

There were about 150 officers and a similar number of NCOs divided altogether into eight platoons each of nearly forty. We had a daily programme of parades, lectures, field work, and demonstrations. Most of the drill done was on the general pattern, but useful enough and always smart. On Saturdays and Sundays we could to into St Omer.

My room companion was F.H. Underhill, 2nd Lt, 1st Herts Regt, a Canadian and a Balliol scholar, and interested in historical matters. One daily event was a 'Quick Think', some small tactical problems to answer for which half a minute was allowed. Answers were marked 'A', 'B' or 'C'. Underhill had 4'B's and 1 'C', and there was only one better, an Australian Captain with 2 'B's only and the rest 'A's. My record for the term included 5 'B's and 1 'C'. Many of the officers were Australians and New Zealanders.

Towards the end of the course there were many competitions and sports for platoon Challenge Cups. I ran in the cross country race of 2½ miles and finished 57th out of 250 starters. I was 12th man in my platoon, and the 12 counted towards the Challenge Cup.

Spent one Saturday afternoon buying Xmas presents for wife and children.

[*Saturday, 15th December*]
Left Wisques and took train at St Omer from Lettinghorn. Marden my servant stayed with my baggage, and I went on to Sallas and lunched with the 17th RB. Afterwards witnessed rugby football match when 17/60th defeated the rest of the Brigade by 8 points to 3. Met other officers of the company and walked back remaining 11 kilos with them to the hamlet of Harlettes.

Our billet, I find, is in a peasant farmer's house where I share a (single) bed with Bunce. The 'A' Co. Mess is in another little farmhouse 100 yards away, and the men are in barns of the usual draughty type, but straw is fairly plentiful. Here we pass our days in morning platoon training and afternoon football matches, etc. until –

[*Xmas Day, 25th December*]
Snow has fallen and it is typical Xmas weather. Only on Xmas Eve a slight thaw melted much of the snow. Wake up late and set out with Scott to gather holly for the decorations. We have taken a roomy little house for the men and picture supplements and holly make the place look very cheery. The men sit down in two batches for a meal of pork, beef, apple sauce, Xmas pudding, fig pudding, apples, beer, and some good cigarettes. Some silver coins gave much pleasure especially to the

aged Madame who sat down to the meal with the men and beams upon one and all. The Brigadier pays us a brief visit.

After dinner, an invitation to the Sergeants' Mess is accepted, and next comes a whist drive for the men. When that is well in progress we have our own dinner of chicken (tough) and Ethel's Xmas pudding. Then back to whist drive and a sing-song to finish the evening.

[Wednesday, 26th December]

Boxing Day. Wake to find inches of snow on the ground and a thunderstorm in progress. We go out for physical training which soon becomes a snowball match. Next a short route march in a driving blizzard. After lunch I settle down to write letters, but am interrupted by 'B' Company officers who have come to challenge the Company to a snow fight. Out we go, and soon our Company rallies, even to cooks in shirt sleeves. After a tough fight 'B' Co. is driven back and dispersed, and all the officers captured except one! At the end we are all so weary we can scarcely squeeze a snowball.

[Thursday, 27th December]

Wake up stiff and sore after the previous day's buffetings. Capt Hankey goes off on leave and hands Company and affairs over to me. Things are in much better order than when I first came out. Lewis gun teams are now trained, also rifle bombers and men are getting to know their work.

Company clearing snow.

[Friday, 28th December]

Capt Hankey goes on leave. Company again on snow clearing. Receive orders for next day's march and learn the dispositions of the Company in going up the line.

[Saturday, 29th December]

Reveille at 3.30 for the men. Get up at 4 a.m., breakfast at 5.20 provided by Madame – eggs and pork, and French bread. I inspect billets, and Company moves off at 6.30 on the road to Wizernes (17 kilos) where we are to entrain. There is a moon and the snow gives some reflected light. A stiff frost and the roads are as bad as possible. A north wind blowing steadily for days has carried the frozen particles like a drifting mist across the fields. Wherever the road is banked drifts of 18 inches to 2 feet have formed right across the track, and often for several hundred yards at a stretch. Through this we plough steadily, at times turning off the road and marching across the open fields. There is small chance of the transport getting through with us. As we advance, we pass Lumbres, and thenceforth the way is better. The roads are in many places cindered.

We reach Wizernes at 11.30; four of my company have dropped behind, but all join up later in the day. The train takes us past Haze-brouck across the Belgian frontier at Abielle, on through Poperinghe and Vlamertinghe, skirting Ypres where the ruins of the Cloth Hall are plainly visible, gaunt and almost shapeless; also the remains of St Martin's Cathedral. On to St Jean, where we detrain.

The Battalion forms up and marches off in file to the Esser Canal, and on the west side of the canal we find a home in the tunnels of Essex Farm. It is dry, about 5ft 6in throughout, and lit with electricity, so we have no complaints to make. Blankets have not arrived, but the tunnels are fairly warm. The men get their own teas, as best they may, for there are several canteens near by. Soon all stretch themselves out to sleep, for they are tired.

[*Sunday, 30th December*]
Awake at 5 a.m. with what I thought was a rat trying to get up my sleeve – probably (from daylight point of view) a mouse! None too warm, but off to sleep again. Had no coat or waterproof sheet with me, but wrap my feet in two old mail bags and cover my hips with two linen maps.

Spend the morning in feet inspection and cleaning up. March off at 2.30 from Essex Farm to Hill Top Farm where we relieve the 1st Dorsets in Reserves. Of course there is no farm to be seen any more than at Essex Farm. But it is difficult to believe that the Bosch formerly held much of the Yser Canal and our line ran back to the railway behind the Canal. Even at this time last year our 18 pdrs[14] were behind the Canal lines. We occupy Nissen huts and the Company settles down therein.

Weather very cold and freezing hard even with a fire in the hut.

[*Monday, 31st December*]
A morning of inspections after a good double on the road to warm the men. Aird goes off to reconnoitre the line up to the supports. Still bitterly cold.

---

[14] Pounders.

A New Year, again in France! I wonder what it will bring for me! But a few days at a time are sufficient nowadays. Go up with CSM Foxwell and Sgt Williams and Randall to reconnoitre the line. A fine keen morning and good going. Seen many tank relics near the St Julien road. A daring Bosch chaser pursues one of our observer planes. Clever diving alone saves our man who gets away within 100 feet of the ground. The Bosch flies off, along our support lines. A good sporting performance on both sides!

[*Wednesday, 2nd January*]
More parades of preparation for the line. Bunce goes off to front line to take over a day in advance, taking Cpl Dollerfield with him – a good NCO who I find is a packer in J. Dickenson & Co.'s paper mills.

[*Thursday, 3rd January*]
An RS officer reached our hut about 1.30 a.m. and reports upon the part of the line we are to take over between Passchendaele and Poelecapelle. His report is favourable and we are cheered up accordingly. A final inspection in the morning and we are ready to move off. Over night a slight thaw has been followed by falls of hail and the ground is frozen stiff once more. We fall in and march off at the appointed intervals. Attached to me and following me close behind is Sapper Clitter of the Field Post Office who has never been under shell-fire nor on a duck-board track before! He is a prospective candidate for a commission.

All goes well until we reach Hubner Farm where we pick up our extras in the way of LGs, water and rations. Here we wait for a quarter of an hour, as it is a light afternoon and the Bosch hold part of the distant ridge. We move off in platoons again and cross the Strombeck bridge. Just as we rise from the little dip, Fritz opens out with 5.9in just ahead of us. Eight shells come in quick succession. They are too near for safety and I give the order to leave the track and scatter for a time in shell-holes.

The shelling continues and comes forward so that the CSM and Sgt Williams have a narrow escape. Gradually we withdraw across the stream and form up beside the rest of the company on the rear slope. For ¾hour the shelling continues and we are lucky to escape without a casualty. One man has left his rifle behind.

Off once more. As we advance we find the track ice-coated and very treacherous. Falls are frequent and on one of these occasions a rum-jar is spilt and wasted – much to the sorrow of the troops! It is a long long

70

journey to the line and it is no consolation to be told that the guide has taken the wrong track. We are taking over from the RBs who have made good arrangements for us. I see each post in turn taken over by our men, though a thick mist and the curious shape of our line makes it difficult to realise our positions.

By 9.15 the relief is complete and I can settle down in my baby elephant dugout for a short rest and a bite of bread and cheese and cup of cocoa, for it is ten hours since the last meal. Freezing hard once more and the mist clears after moon-rise.

[Friday, 4th January]

Turn out again at 3 a.m. and issue rum ration to all the posts. Now bright moonlight. We are interrupted several times by long-range whiz-bangs, which fall close, but the shooting is erratic, and merely searching in design. Return to the dugout about 4.30 a.m. and settle down to sleep until about 10 a.m. Wake up to a fine morning and lie under the blankets we have brought whilst Bunce as an old campaigner sets to work to boil water and fry sausages!

It is impossible to show a head above ground, so our servant who is 25 yards away is not available until night-fall. An excellent breakfast! Lie in 'bed' and write up diary. Just before going into line have read a letter from Clara speaking of Father's great weakness, and am anxious accordingly.

We are in a fine commanding position, but the Bosch still holds high ground away to the E. It is a curious outlook with Bosch concrete dugouts looming up at intervals. Two aeroplanes form a landmark a few hundred yards apart – one British and one Bosch, each with tail upturned and nose imbedded deep in the mud. Not a Bosch to be seen. His Very lights go up 500 yards away where he is probably working hard on new lines of defence. His patrols come out close to our lines at times.

Inside it is curious to sit or lie all day in a little tunnel closed at one end, or cave as one might call it, 3ft high and 10ft long, built up of sandbags roofed with light corrugated steel. One gazes out on a bank of frozen earth and watches the shadow slowly climb the bank of earth as the sun gets lower. Bosch aeroplanes have been over this morning, and the result is seen when we are whiz-banged from long range at intervals of about an hour and a half for the next day and a half.

At dusk visit front line and have just returned when Major Fairlie arrives. Accompany him to front line and inspect the posts. Meanwhile Bunce and two other ranks are out on patrol. It is a dark night and not easy to find our eight shell-hole posts which we examine carefully and critically, also the wire in front.

It is now –

Return to HQ and turn out once more to visit the posts and meet the MG officer at 'B' Company quarters. As we enter No. 4 Post we are greeted with a burst of MG fire and the bullets whistle just over my head. A Lewis gunner who is standing by his gun is hit and falls silently save for slight moaning. Our Lewis guns reply and the Bosch withdraws. Wright of No. 3 Platoon is the man hit. I return to Co. HQ for stretcher-bearers, and learn that the man died within a quarter of an hour. He was buried by his comrades near Sourd Farm and a rough cross marks his grave.

It is now 5 a.m. We turn in and sleep until 1 p.m. when Bunce again cooks our dejourner [sic]. Fritz is now strafing with whiz-bangs again and his aim is good. Our coffee is just boiling when a shell pitches 10 yards off. Realising what is coming I call to Bunce, 'Quick! pull the coffee in.' Just in time the coffee is snatched inside, as a shower of ice and mud falls on the spot where it had stood. At dusk we stir out once more, making our arrangements for a company relief. 'C' Company is to take over our posts and we to retire to Support Lines. Capt Harvey of 'C' Company arrives about 6 p.m.

Meanwhile Bunce is once more out on patrol but the night is so dark that nothing is to be seen of the enemy. Several of his patrols are to be heard and on our left they endeavour to rush one of our posts. A Sgt-Major jumps into the post and falls on to the bayonet of one of our men. The other Bosch turns tail and the Sgt-Major is taken prisoner. It is 11 p.m. before the relief is complete and we are in our new quarters in the Support Lines.

Wake to sharp frost once more. 'Stand to' at 6.30, and go round with rum issue. The 4 platoons are widely separated, in trenches and small dugouts. On the sides of the tracks there are many remains of the offensive of July 31st when this ground was won. We are at Vacher Farm and CHQ. Here there are gruesome traces of the Jocks who made their advance with packs on their backs and lost many men in the mud.

We remain quiet by day. About 3 p.m. an air fight is in progress above us. There's a shout of 'There's one down!' I am too late to see the descent, but down came a Bosch monoplane with engine still running. It crashes down only 300 or 400 yards from us, narrowly missing a MG post and tiny dugout. The pilot had been shot through the head. The engine buries itself 3 or 4 feet in the ground and the remainder of the machine is but a tangled mass of wood spars and linen. Some Sussex officers are in the dugout with us at the time and are early on the scene. They tell us that two Artillery officers have taken from the machine

72

everything worth having. I receive instructions from BHQ that the machine is in my area and thereupon inspect it and place a guard over it. Everything of value has been taken but I find out and report the number of the Battery to which the Artillery officers belong. We bury the airman, and Aird makes a cross for his grave, with the inscription: 'W.B. . . . , an unknown German airman shot down 6.1.18. RIP'. It is the best we can do for a man who after all is a gallant foeman. Even that inscription seems a contrast to the many unknown men of our side who lie half buried around.

[*Monday, 7th January*]
In the early morning we receive a visit from three officers of the RFC sent to investigate. From a label on the wing '3.9.17' they describe the machine as an Albatross III and are satisfied without seeing the machine, which they had tramped all night to view!

It is the morning of our relief. As the morning advances a thaw sets in and most of the snow disappears. In the afternoon our CO appears with the CO of the Cambridgeshires who are to relieve us. I get a strafing for the untidy state round the trenches. Probably well deserved, but I was not allowing them to come out to clear us the mess which the thaw disclosed before dusk fell. Before we left the place was set in good order.

First relieving parties arrive about 5 p.m. It is well after 7 p.m. before I can report by telephone the relief complete. My key word is 'January', and calling up the Adjutant I ask 'Is my leave due in January?' I am not understood, but my thrust seems to have got home, for by the time I report at BHQ in person the Adjutant is laughing heartily at the sally. We make our way with the traditional duckboard 'crawl' to the soup kitchen, where we have a tiresome wait of two hours for the train. But of men coming out of the line nothing damps the spirits. They form up in groups and circles and sing and dance literally in ecstatic mood, so great is the reaction to the strain of shell-fire.

Then we board the train, and move off in open trucks for Siege Camp on the road between Vlamertinghe and Elverdinghe. It is bitterly cold, but there is no thought of complaint. We are quartered in Nissen huts, comfortable enough if only fuel is forthcoming. On reaching camp I get a telegram sent off on the Thursday morning telling me of my old father's serious condition. There is also a letter from Clara, and armed with these I make on . . .

[*Tuesday, 8th January*]

. . . an application for early leave. We wake to find four inches of snow on the ground and carry out a limited programme of Company training. The post brings me a letter from my dear wife telling me of the death on the Friday of my old father. It is a sorrow not to see his face again, but I feel a real relief that he was spared long suffering hours such as my dear mother endured.

[*Wednesday, 9th January*]

A morning of Company training and then off after lunch, with my leave warrant, homewards! The thought of home brings joy that blots out all trace of sorrow for the time. It is difficult to realise the loss I have sustained – a bath, tea, and dinner in Poperinghe, and I find Anderson of the Scottish Rifles and IInd Army School, at the Officers' Club at Poperinghe.

[*Thursday, 10th January*]

We wait on the platform on Pop. Stn for the 1.26 train which runs in an hour late. Fairly comfortable journey down to Calais. Breakfast at the Officers' Club, a wash and shave, an early lunch, and then on board at 1.15 p.m. Blighty Bound.

A choppy crossing and I am much exercised in the 1½ hours of the trip. Soon recover in the Pullman car at the Victoria train. Arrive at 6.47 p.m. A dash for a taxi, off to Waterloo. Catch the 7.0 train with a minute to spare. On the platform awaiting me, my dear wife. Home once more! My dear old father's funeral was on Wednesday.

3

March 1918: The German Attack

[*Thursday, 21st March 1918*]
We of the 17th KRRC are now in General Headquarters Reserve, and quartered at Sorel-le-Grand in the usual Nissen (Bow) huts. We are 3 miles due west of Vaucelette Farm, our outpost line which we had occupied for nearly the whole of February, and are midway between Gouzeancourt and Epéhy, which lie 10 miles SSE of Cambrai. We are, it seems, one of three Divisions in Reserve, out of the 14 Divisions which comprise the Fifth Army. We are engaged each day in working parties, and the rumours of the coming great German offensive are so frequent that we attach less importance to them than we did on the 15th and 16th March when we were occupying trenches in the rear of Gouzeancourt. But the statement of a prisoner on the morning of the 20th gives rise to fresh rumour. Our working party for that morning is cancelled and we are sent hastily to dig a switch trench in the Gouzeancourt district. In this work Mr Winston Churchill,[1] the Duke of Westminster and the GOC take the greatest interest. (Winston, who can never be like other mortals, wears a trench helmet; the Duke of Westminster is content with a cloth cap, though well inside the tin hat compulsory area.) Overnight we go to bed with a dim notion of the possibilities of the morrow, but with no special preparations for a 'stand to'.

It is 4.30 a.m. of the 21st when we are awakened by a bombardment, and its intensity leaves no room for doubting its purpose. With a feeling of suppressed excitement we are out of bed and dressing quickly, amid a round of mutual chaff and banter in our officers' huts. Shrapnel is already bursting heavily over the village and the word is passed to assemble in the valley on the football field, which is almost 'dead' ground. Here we fall in by platoons in the darkness, only to find that 14 of our men have already been hit in the huts by shrapnel. In fact, No. 4 Platoon of our 'A' Company is reduced to a Lewis gun team only.

[1] On 25th March Churchill visited the front near Noules with the Duke of Westminster and General Tudor, GOC Ninth Division. The next morning, the German bombardment was, wrote Churchill, 'The most tremendous canonade I shall ever hear' (Martin Gilbert, *Winston Churchill*, vol. iv, Heinemann 1975).

Leppan[2] (a South African) is in command of 'A' Company. I take
No. 3 Platoon 24 strong, under Sergeant Randle, MM, a stout fellow –
once left for dead by the Turks! He comes of a Nuneaton mining family,
in civil life is a barman, ready and genial, and a good man for any
emergency. Scott takes No. 1 Platoon, and Bunce goes to No. 2 with
the remnants of No. 4 Platoon. Aird is still at the Army School, and
McCulloch at the Reinforcement Camp. Our CO, Col Le Prevost, DSO
is Acting Brigadier. Major Fairlie is in Command of the Battalion and
moves about 'strafing' everyone impartially in a firm and soldierly
manner. This seems to be the correct thing to do on such occasions,
and on the whole the effect is good.

Presently we move back to Battalion Headquarters, where Regimental
Sergeant-Major Hawkswell with be-ribboned breast (hence familiarly
known to the men as 'Rainbow') is serving out spare bandoliers of
ammunition, bombs and rifle grenades. Rations of bully, biscuits, tea
and sugar, and cheese are also issued, and the men get a bit of food
before moving off by Platoons to our Assembly point at Sorrel Wood,
a mile and a half away. We avoid the village and go direct through the
mist across the Downs, making for the valley edge of the wood. 'A'
Company is there first, without any mishap, but with the uncomfortable
feeling that we may walk into gas shelling at any moment. We lie down
by platoons on the 'dead' side of the valley – the slope nearest to the
enemy. 'C' and 'D' Companies are just arriving. There is a whizz of
heavy shells, and two or three fall among the approaching platoon
groups. When the smoke clears, several khaki figures lie dotted on the
slopes amid the mist, and the repeated call for 'Stretcher-bearers' tells
its tale. For safety sake we move our platoons further from the wood.
The mist hangs on. It is broad daylight now and blue sky shows overhead, giving occasional glimpses of an observation balloon just in front
of us. Bursts of shrapnel seem to be directed at this, and some falls in
our valley. Meanwhile our Transport and Battalion Headquarters has
established itself in a pocket of the valley on the backward slope behind
us. A Bosch aeroplane, like some great humming-bird moth, flits out
of the mist in the attempt to fire the balloon. The attempt fails. A few
minutes and a heavy shell pitches just beyond our assembled field
cookers, for the enemy aeroplane has noted the dark patches on the
hillside. There is a hasty withdrawal; the galloping cookers with their
steaming boilers are only just in time, for shells follow in quick succession. We all move a short distance along the valley, and hastily dig
deep and narrow slit trenches for protection. These are just complete
when there is a whirring, humming sound. A Bosch aeroplane – four
or five more appear out of the mist above the sausage balloon. One

[2] Leppan was awarded the MC for his part in the subsequent fighting.

hovers; dives with a splutter of machine-gun bullets – tracer bullets that leave a trail of white smoke. Missed! By Jove! But the balloon is doomed! Another aeroplane hovers a moment right above its prey; swoops and turns. There is a thin trail of white smoke, then a burst of black fumes, and slowly the balloon descends a flaming mass. Apparently it is but a dummy, for there is no parachute descent from the dependent car, which falls lightly to the ground.

Once more we move and proceed to dig again. My faithful servant, Marden, helps me to dig in the chalk an armchair hole for the two of us, and we line it with dry grass. This is just ready, when the word comes to assemble at the top of the ridge nearer the enemy, as the Battalion is about to march off. Meanwhile news has come through of the capture of Vaucelette Farm by the Bosch, who has penetrated to Railton (Box Dump) but is isolated there. He has captured Chapel Crossing, but been thrown out again by the South African Scottish. (At Vaucelette Farm facing Villers Guislain and Gonnelieu, our Battalion spent the month of February, and the Bosch offensive was expected at that time. We were an outpost line, with orders to hold on 'for duration'; there was to be no withdrawing from trench to trench. About half way through the month the orders were changed. The British barrage, when the 'SOS' signal was given, would descend on the outpost line, and the garrison had permission to withdraw 'through the *gaps* in the barrage'. This did not sound very hopeful, particularly as the Artillery knew nothing of any barrage gaps! We were profoundly thankful not to try the experiment.) So much we know, and there are big rumours of British offensives at Passchendaele, at Lens, and where not? The French 'have made a big push at Verdun'! So does rumour feed the tired Tommy.

All the morning, up to midday, the ground has throbbed and quivered with the heavy Artillery. Amid it all the larks are singing overhead! For the afternoon the sound is less heard, save far to the north. The heavy mist continues to favour the Bosch attack. Our Battalion's casualties for the day number nearly fifty, all caused by the shelling of the early morning. Fortunately few of the men are killed, and of the 14 men hit in our own Company all but two have light flesh wounds.

The Battalion assembles under the shelter of a high bank whilst an officer and various NCOs go forward to reconnoitre. Then about 6.30 p.m. we march off in file going SW to occupy a post in the brown (or third) line of defence. There is something wrong with our guidance, for on and on we trudge, and though the distance is said not to be great we seem to be going in circles. It is 2.30 a.m. before we reach a line of trenches, partly dug, on which the Gloucester Pioneers are still at work.

Honour Satisfied

The Bosch break through south of us. 'A' Company is told off for the
support lines, and I am sent to choose a site for a trench or line of posts
yet to be dug. About 150 yards in rear of our brown trench I find a low
bank, running parallel with the main road to Longavesnes, another 150
yards in rear. This serves our purpose, and on top of the bank we begin
to dig ourselves in for the night. Daylight comes, with another thick
mist, and a heavy bombardment opens once again in the near distance.
Shells for the guns and supplies have been moving forward unceasingly,
and the German shelling by night has been less heavy than we expected.
Soon after daylight a trickle of wounded and stragglers appears upon
the road, and we learn by degrees a little of what is happening. The
Bosch had found his way on the previous day into Epéhy – our old
familiar spot – but had been removed by the efforts of our own 118th
Brigade. A stalwart Company Sergeant-Major of the Munsters – his
breast ablaze with ribbons – tells us he could do no more in Epéhy
(which seems to have fallen once more), and he had got away that
morning with a handful of men. The mist begins to lift and reveals us
our position. We are at the extreme loop of a hairpin bend in the line,
with a fine frontal fire down a long but narrow valley. On our right the
trenches bend sharply over a ridge, held by the Rifle Brigade, and we
do not like the look of this hidden flank. Of that more later. Our horizon
in front is a long ridge (near Villers Faucon) perhaps two miles distant,
under the crest of which runs our yellow (or second) line, for here we
can see the burst of enemy shells. Half-left is the village of Sulcourt
which held our Brigade Headquarters early in the day, but was afterwards shelled by both sides impartially. A few tanks seem to be moving
southwards under cover of the ridge. Meanwhile stragglers continue.
We seem to be placed ready to hold up an attack so I determine to find
a rifle. I head off one rough looking fellow, who tells me he has been
'gassed and buried', and is off to a dressing-station. He wishes to take
his rifle with him. But I tell him a rifle is worth more in 'the line' than
at a dressing-station. I get my rifle and he continues his way – at a pace
the envy of one who has been neither gassed nor buried! We are settling
down in our trench and watching the gradual approach of the enemy
shelling, when a message arrives that an officer and one NCO per platoon
is to go back to reconnoitre a line (the green line) in Tincourt Wood.
Apparently this means that the enemy is breaking through on one of
the flanks; probably the right. I am told off for the job and take my
servant, Marden, and 4 NCOs with me. Battalion Headquarters are now
in some huts on the road to Longavesnes. Here I find our CO as
Brigadier, our Second in Command and the various Staff Officers in
consultation, and I await the arrival of an officer from each of the other
Companies. We have had no food all day, so I am fain to beg some

biscuits from some Engineers near by, and fill my pockets with a store for future use. As we move off Major Fairlie urges me to leave my trench coat and lining, which I carry in addition to the leather jerkin I am wearing – 'for', he says, 'you will return here'! It is now very warm in the sun, but I decline with thanks, and the event proves that I am right. We move off down the road to Longavesnes, wedged tight in a long stream of wounded men, all helping or being helped in turn. As we reach the village the enemy 5.9s begin to search it, or maybe seek to deal with some tanks which are drawing out of the rear side. One shell drops unpleasantly close to our sides, and only an intervening wall saved us from the fragments. We turn off sharply through some neat little military gardens, and strike across the open ground towards the steep, blunt-nosed chalk hill, the end of a spur, on top of which lies Tincourt Wood. 'A' and 'B' Companies are to occupy the forward edge of the wood, with 'A' on the south, and 'B' on the north. I go to examine our quarters and am warned to be careful about stepping out of the wood, for three Sussex men have already been 'sniped' in crossing the little lane. The danger is probably exaggerated but I make a some-what gingerly survey of the lines, which are obvious enough within the wood. As we prepare to return, low-flying enemy aircraft appear and with their machine guns try to make things unpleasant for us. We return by the southern road, and before we strike the village we find ourselves vigorously sniped at from the hill-sides, and it becomes increasingly difficult to understand the position of affairs! In the village itself a field gun is making any movement very unpleasant, as the shells fired with a very low trajectory are sweeping it through and through. I make for the north of the village, being the quietest side, and even then the snipers are hitting the banks and walls uncomfortably near by. Marden is with me, but I have got ahead of my NCOs who have waited to get some water from a cart. At last we are on the main road, clear of the village, but the sniping follows us closely. I realise that my duty is to get back to my Battalion and make my report as soon as possible, and so we dodge by leaps and bounds from one heap of stones to another. The Bosch are now shelling the huts where Battalion Headquarters had been, and I am beginning to wonder where I shall make my report. A body of troops appears coming in the distance down the road. These prove to be our own Battalion, led by the Adjutant, and I rejoin them and act as guide. Giving the village a wide berth, we pass to the north, and make our way up the slope of the hills. The men then lie down to rest whilst we reconnoitre once more. Meanwhile Bosch aeroplanes are again very busy overhead. By this time all are hungry, thirsty, footsore and weary, but we are promised that rations shall reach us during the night! Our men improve their time of resting in the wood by examining some empty tents. To their delight they find cheese, jam, marmalade,

butter and even eggs, and soon their hunger is appeased, and I and
other officers are not forgotten. Eventually by comparison of orders
received, a working plan is formed for the defence of the hill. The
Cheshires take the front line with our 'B' Company on their left, and
the remnants of our 'C' and 'D' Companies stretching down into the
valley to the north where they in turn join up with other troops. The
southern and rearward slopes of the hill are held by the Black Watch
and the Sussex and as the event proved the full weight of the Bosch
attack fell here, and here our line was broken. But of that later. 'A'
Company is in support, in a deep but very wide trench, in which we
prepare suitable fire-steps. This is an improvement upon an earlier
arrangement whereby 'A' Company were in support in a shallow trench
within the wood, wherein it is not possible even to stand upright, so
closely is it swept by machine-gun fire. We settle down for the night.
By the way there is no wire in front of any of these trenches, only on
the red and yellow lines which the Bosch has already won.

Now it is well to go back a bit to learn what has happened in the
brown line during my absence. It seems that the enemy artillery fire
crept closer and closer, until shells were falling in and around our own
trenches. There was no direct attack in front, until word was passed by
the Rifle Brigade that the Bosch were coming in on the right, and were
actually pushing down the trench, to pour later over the little ridge
already mentioned with misgiving. What happened next I do not know.
There was some heavy fighting in which Wallace and Peppler ('C'
Company, a Winchester officer) were wounded, and got away. McIntyre
and Capt Hervey of 'C' Company were wounded and left as prisoners.
Of 'C' and 'D' Companies few men escaped, and the missing for a time
included Cpl Fuller and a Lewis gun team of 'A' Company, most of
whom fortunately rejoined us later, after spending a night in the same
village as the Bosch. Scott of my own ('A') Company got orders to
withdraw, just in time to avoid being surrounded. He was the last to
leave and was heavily sniped at. Late that evening we still heard distant
rifle fire, but that was the last effort. The 16th RBs were badly cut up;
the 17th Sherwoods on our left suffered likewise, and lost their CO,
and 'A' Company KRR was thenceforth the only substantial body in
the Brigade. Our Company strength at this stage was 3 officers and 85
ORs.[3] (Bunce[4] was already attached to 'B' Company.)

Night comes on with us in our support trenches, not too badly placed,
and ready for an attack on the morrow. Burning huts and villages on
either side tell their tale of the Bosch advance. There are several 'alarms'
due to Bosch patrols, Bunce on the sunken road to our left is at times

[3] Other ranks.
[4] Lieutenant Bunce appears frequently in these pages. He survived the war but was not decorated.

busy in bombing the enemy out of some huts, under cover of which the wily Bosch is creeping up. I dig myself a small seat in the left hand bay of our line, held by my platoon. There is a gap between us and 'B' Company and I prefer to be on this spot to await possible developments. I snatch an hour or two's sleep at odd times. Fortunately the nights are not too cold, and the extra clothing I am carrying serves me well in rest hours.

The contrast between our present position and the lines we used to hold in the Ypres Salient is well shown by the reply of our Artillery to an 'SOS' signal. On the approach of a Bosch patrol the Cheshires fire a three-red light (the 'SOS') signal from our front line. In the Ypres Salient within half a minute a tempest of shells would have burst in front of us. Here we wait a full minute in expectancy. Then there comes one solitary 18-pounder shell! Thenceforth we determine to rely upon our Lewis guns and rifles alone!

A remark dropped by an officer of the Sussex throws a side light upon my trials and troubles in returning through Longavesnes village on the previous afternoon. He said he had been sending reports to his Brigade Headquarters that the Bosches held the village, and probably some if not most of the heavy sniping came from our own men on the hill sides! If only he had had a good pair of glasses he might have known better.

[*Saturday, 23rd March*]

The Fog Battle. We have an early 'Stand to' in readiness for the expected attack, and have time to examine our position in the growing dawn. 'A' Company is in support, and therefore has no field of fire so long as the front trench holds. We face down the blunt nose of the hill, looking towards the village of Longavesnes and the long valley down which we had come the previous day. On our right is Tincourt Wood round the outskirts of which sweeps our front line of trenches. All that happens here is out of our view. Away to the left (north) is a deep, fairly wide valley, cut by good lines of trenches which head across to the ridge on our left, where they are lost behind the sky line. As the daylight strengthens there are no signs of fog, and all ask for nothing better than the position they hold, even in the absence of protective wire.

Soon the Bosch can be seen massing in the village behind some huts. Our field guns have seen them too, and begin to pour shrapnel into the solid ranks. Through my glasses I can see the foremost skirmishers creep forward, and in twos and threes dash for the horse lines to the north of the village, through which we had walked the previous afternoon. Gradually they mass here under cover of a protecting bank. Now the sun appears. And with it a few puffs or wisps of mist. Quickly this spreads and settles down over all. Once again our advantage is gone and we are to fight after all in an enveloping fog. Anxiously we wait, knowing that the Bosch can now mass his men as he chooses and launch them when and where he likes. Random fire into a wall of mist is but a waste of precious cartridges.

Soon there is a sputter of rifle fire from below, bursting later into an intermittent rattle, and swelling at times with sudden burst of rapid fire. A steady bombardment is kept up by two or three 18-pounders on our behalf, and a few enemy whiz-bangs fall around and about us. But artillery is out of the hunt in to-day's reckoning, wherein numbers and weight of attack or defence will decide the issue.

The firing in the valley below increases. A runner arrives with a note for 'A' Company asking for reinforcements. Leppan orders me to take my platoon to the support of 'D' Company. Sergeant Randle and I exchange glances, for we guess we are to fill a tight corner. We examine rifles once again to see that bolts are in working order; each man carries spare ammunition, and with swords[5] fixed we file down the sunken road into the valley. There we find Barber of 'D' Company with a dozen or so men lining a low bank which runs diagonally to the front. He asks me to take his place here whilst he pushes his men forward, and to watch his flank which seems to rest on a road and track leading towards the village. My men line the bank, and I send Cpl Donafield and four men to watch the upper track on our right. Meanwhile the firing in front seems to be slackening. In the thick mist it is difficult to know what is actually happening. A tank comes lumbering out of the mist and squats down, snorting and spitting bullets, just behind us. Enemy machine guns are playing down the valley, and the bullets 'rico' merrily from the armoured sides of the tank. I walk up to this tank. A shutter opens in front and a white face appears at the open port-hole. It is the officer in charge whose appearance is made the more curious by protective spectacles made up of tiny dangling chains, forming a shiny fringe, which ward off splinters from the eyes. Two more tanks come galumping through the mist, one cruising madly in the wrong direction. I stand up and question the pilot who owns that he has waltzed round so many times that he hasn't an earthly notion where he is. What can he best do? So I send him off gaily up the road where our men had led. Just now we are being pretty heavily 'whiz-banged' and are bespattered with the mud and earth displaced by the shells. Probably it is our own artillery falling short, though should the mist lift we shall have a hot time in the centre of a triangle formed by three tanks! Major Fairlie, our CO appears, strolling quietly about all by himself. He expresses satisfaction with what has been done, but asks me to push my Lewis gun post up a little. So I go forward a hundred yards and find a snug

---

[5] 'Sword' is the rifleman's term for bayonet.

spot which the Lewis gun team fills. Next I meet Major Wingfield (attached to us from the Gloucester Pioneers), much occupied in dodging the whiz-bangs and machine-gun bullets (which have already passed him!) but for all that carrying out his duties to the letter. He tells me that if we get the order to retire, we fall back in the direction of Moislains, where two months before we had passed a night, and take up a line between villages of Aizecourt and Bussu, NE of Peronne. But we seem to have done our work on this bit of front, and a retirement at the moment is surely very remote.

In a few minutes, as the mist shows signs of lifting. I receive a written order from Leppan to withdraw SW in the direction already named. It is amazing news! But we learn that the Black Watch line to our south is pierced, and that the Bosch is working round behind us on the right.

I set my compass to give the general direction in the fog, form up the men and march off as ordered. At the SW corner of Tincourt Wood we find the CO and Adjutant, and a group of others round a stretcher. On this lies poor Freer, badly shot through neck and shoulder; he was acting as liaison officer and was standing by Major Fairlie when he was hit. We have 600 or 700 yards of open country to cross; before we gain the shelter of a wood we come under machine-gun fire from the flanking ridge which the Bosch has won. Once in the wood we halt to decide our plan of action. Peering round with my glasses I am glad to find Leppan and the rest of 'A' Company following not far in our rear, and with them we join forces. Once outside the wood we are in 'dead' ground and leading directly SW in the direction of Bussu. We avoid the main road, now thronged with detachments of troops all in full retreat. Our caution is rewarded, for the enemy 'heavies' soon wake up and begin an accurate search of the road. We hurry our steps; there is never any need to urge men on when heavy shell fire can be avoided. Bosch 8in shells are falling every minute along the road, which a Bosch field gun is also enfilading from the ridge on our left. The open country-side is now streaked with long trails of men retiring in fair order on Bussu. We are in sight of the village when the enemy heavy artillery settles down upon it, and the small garrison must be having a terrible time, as roofs and houses are pounded to bits. We draw away to the south of the valley, and rest in 'dead' ground, under the shelter of a steep bank. But only for a few minutes, and we push on once more to our halting place, a wood half a mile down the valley, where our Battalion is to re-form. On the way along we have passed men of the Sussex and other Battalions entrenched in prepared positions, and ready to defend the road and fight a rearguard action until all the troops from the forward area are clear. It will shortly be our duty in turn to carry out the same programme; tired and sleepy we are already. It is grillingly hot and dusty as we drag ourselves wearily along. It is not yet midday.

On comparing notes, we find that Fifield of 'C' Company, who was with me at Tincourt Wood the day before, has been killed by a shell – probably our own. The Bosch pressed on right up to the 'B' Company trenches on the northern slope of the hill. Here he was enfiladed by a Lewis gun and left some 30 dead in front of our trench. Bunce has again been busily bombing the Bosch out of the huts near the sunken road, halfway down towards the valley. Nowhere did the Bosch gain a footing in our trenches.

The sun is now grillingly hot, as we file slowly to take up shell-hole positions to form a defensive flank to the main Peronne road on its southern side. Apparently we are working on a time-table, for the Bosches are only just appearing over the slopes 2,000 yards away when we move once more to a line covering Mt St Quentin, and to the north of the Allsines – Bussu railway. Here a pause, whilst machine guns engage the distant enemy and delay his advance. It is all splendid, defensive country, open and with a fine field of fire, and looking upon our own little bit, it seems a mystery that we are not to stop to defend it.

Back we march once more, now turning, under shrapnel fire, towards Mt St Quentin, the fine hill-top which seems to form a natural defence for Peronne. Here we see the British Tommy at his irrepressible best. Tired and worn, he pauses for a rest. Some bright spirit lights upon a quartermaster's store filled with all manner of change of raiment. Lo! the Bosch is but 2,000 yards away and coming on fast. But Tommy strips him[self] stark-naked, and shouts with glee as he dons clean vest, shirt, pants and socks, and what not. One man has an armful of clean towels which he doles out in official style to every man who passes. I gladly accept the offer of a new pair of socks, and a boon they prove, for my feet are already blistered and painful.

Down the rearward slope of Mt St Quentin we trudge, and turn the first to the right down the Cléry road. We skirt Peronne and halt, on the deep sunken road which runs N. and S., to form a bridgehead guard. The village of Allaines(?) is all ablaze, and in many quarters the oncoming of the Bosch is to be traced in the smoke columns that darken the sky.

Meanwhile there are masses of our transport and artillery limbers parked on the slopes towards Cléry. Now the Bosch heavy artillery has got the range. The fall of heavy shells amid the struggling mass of horses and men is one of the wickedest sights of the day! Most of the limbers gallop clear away. But scores of smashed carts and wheels and many a fallen horse and team repay the Bosch for their ghastly efforts.

We are wondering what our defence of the bridgehead may mean, when – a rending z-zoom and fragments of bridge fly 100 or 200 feet into the air, all falling nearly on the same spot. Our work is done for the time being. We fall in once more, and lead across the marshy land by a beaten track in the direction of Cléry. On this track all the troops mingle in one confused stream. But once across we reform and our Brigade mans a line of trenches covering the main road and firing occasionally at the distant Bosch who is now coming over Mt St Quentin, from which our men are retiring steadily. The advance of the Bosch is followed by his many aeroplanes, to whom he signals his position by means of white Very lights; of these he seems to carry an unending supply, and his plan works well. We hold our trench whilst the road behind us is cleared of miles and miles of motor and horse transport, and some half a dozen tanks which roll lazily away, steaming and snorting loudly.

When all is clear, we receive the word to quit the trench and cross the road. By this time a Bosch machine gun has cleverly hit off the range, and we are finely chased to the nearest cover. Here Bosch aeroplanes (perhaps a dozen) take up the running and we scurry in ignominious flight to re-form under cover at the foot of the slope leading towards the bridges of Cléry. Several of our men have been hit by the machine-gunners in the aeroplanes, mostly leg wounds. (There is an uncomfortable feeling about standing in the open under aeroplane fire, but except against mass targets the effect of the fire is merely distracting – almost negligible in its results.) By the roadside we pass two tanks which have run out of petrol, and the crew are preparing to burn them. Our 'boys' pick up a chicken, a ham and some bottles of wine from a Headquarters limber abandoned by the roadside.

But our troubles are not yet over – our course in the Peronne Handicap is not yet run to a finish. The Bosch have not been idle and have a good eye for country. They have mounted a field gun on high ground about 2,000 yards east of us, and can enfilade the road and approaches to the Cléry bridges with direct fire and open sights. At present they are firing about two shots to the minute. We draw in to a covering chalk-pit to examine their methods and the best escape. Soon they turn their attention to the plank bridges which span the streams, under which the current is flowing swiftly. We watch others run the gauntlet of shots. One shell skims the heads of two tall men and falls 'plonk' in the water ten yards beyond, splashing all with mud and water. The tall men are our CO, Major Fairlie, and Scott of 'A' Company, as I afterwards learn. The next shell bursts in the bank, and a man doubles up – badly hit, as we can see. He proves to be Jones, one of the stoutest of our corporals. Quickly we realise what a direct hit on a bridge will mean – that we shall have to swim for it! The next shell pitches among some men clustered in a corner under the lea of the cliff which we are hugging. Another sets light to some huts near by. There is no time to lose! We make our dash – safely as it proves. We come upon our injured man

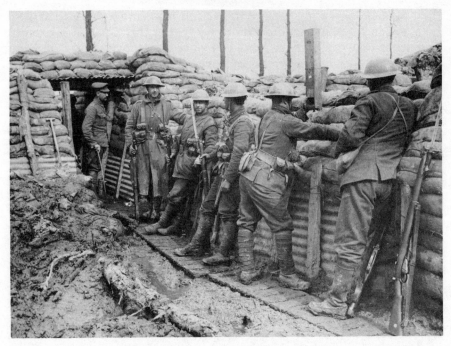

Riflemen in a trench with periscope.

whom an artilleryman is binding up. It is our Cpl Jones in a sorry plight, with shrapnel in the neck, back, arms and legs. There are three sergeants with me, two of whom carry poor Jones, whilst Sgt Williams and I bring along two rifles apiece. Now we can move leisurely and we collect the stragglers of our Company and bring them slowly along through some orchards to the canal bank. Here we cross the bridge to the southern bank and find our Staff Captain who tells us where the Brigade will form up. Our 'A' Company is 75 strong, with rifles and ammunition, Lewis guns and nearly all panniers complete – a creditable record after a harassing, demoralising day. Headquarters and the other three companies muster 70 between them, and we are then the strongest Battalion in the Brigade. The 16th Rifle Brigade, I believe, totalled about 30 men, and the 17th Sherwood Foresters between 40 and 50.

But our work is not yet done. Darkness is coming on as we are led off to line a trench for the defence of the canal should the enemy attempt to follow up his success. A series of explosions just as darkness comes on tells the tale of the blowing up of the Cléry bridges, all built with wooden beams, and the glare from burning timbers seems to show that the destruction is complete. Fritz has done well this day, but must be just as 'played out' as we are. We settle down in a dry and fairly comfortable trench and I am just asleep, when the blinking of a flash lamp pronounces that all is 'OK' in the direction of the bridges, and soon word comes that we are to be relieved. Off we march by road to a large hut, close to the canal bridge of Feuilleres, 2½ miles to the west of Cléry. Here about mid-night we settle down to a real rest – officers and men all in the same hut. I sleep warmly and well for five or six hours.

One incident must be recorded as showing the true character of the British Tommy. There is a man in 'A' Company, a great, strong, hulking fellow, but an inveterate grumbler, one who 'grouses' loudly whenever he is not otherwise employed. When Freer was hit, stretcher-bearers were needed, and Peronne was eight miles away. Our Scotsman – for such he was – was there unasked, and helped to carry his officer those eight long miles, and without a murmur! I feel pleased now that I judged the man's character aright. For hearing his 'grousing' in the darkness one night I said to him, 'You are just the man I like to hear. For I know well enough that if old Fritz came over the top at us, you would be the first man out and after him!' The other men laughed at the time; now the man has proved himself and in an even better way than I could have hoped.

[*Sunday, 24th March*]

Guarding the Somme bridges. We are awake at daylight after five or six hours of splendid rest. Our cookers or at least two of them have arrived and prepare a good hot breakfast. Curiously enough 'A' Company cooks managed to elude the Bosch; the 'C' and 'D' cooks were not so fortunate. 'A' Company's cooker was captured on the afternoon of the second day, but the cooks get away with another Company's cooker, and their arrival is warmly welcomed. A light mist still shields us, and we scatter and lie resting in old shell-holes in some orchards near by. We are near the Canal de la Somme, and gradually realise that we are to be the bridge-head guard at Feuilleres in which tiny village we are lying, just south of the canal, not more than a stone's throw beyond which flows the river, here shallow and divided into several streams. We rest contentedly until about 10 a.m. when the mist lifts, and enemy aircraft begin to be busy overhead. Orders arrive that we are to take up a position covering the bridges, and we find some old trenches, excellently sited for bringing a cross fire to bear upon the canal bridge and approaches. These we occupy. Next we get orders to line the canal bank itself. Here the field of fire is less good, but we are well screened by a long row of old apple trees, and gradually make our men inconspicuous in shallow rifle pits dug in the bank and camouflaged with grass and branches of trees. The trouble is that one cannot dig to any depth, or water appears at once.

87

At this point the canal runs due east and west, so that we are forming a defensive flank, gazing in enfilade at the trenches our men still hold on the bold sweep of hills which rise from the northern bank of the river. 'And all day long the noise of battle rolls' – is the line from the 'Morte D'Arthur' which keeps running through my mind. There is heavy fighting in progress across the river, away to the NE. Gradually the shelling draws nearer and it is plain that slowly our men are withdrawing westwards. Soon we are within machine-gun range – say 2,500 yards, and we wonder what work will fall to our lot! Then comes word that the 1st Division has counter-attacked (after taking over from the 41st Division) and has driven the Bosch back in fine style. Our spirits revive wonderfully, and the enemy shelling is undoubtedly more distant. The 118th Brigade (39th Division) in the morning have been sent down to Herbecourt. In the afternoon they return by another route, and are thrown across the bridge to take a spell of rearguard work. Tired as they are the double march seems an unnecessary hardship. Can it be a piece of bluff on the part of our Staff? – to give the impression that fresh troops are being moved up! In the afternoon Gen Feetham who commands our (39th) Division appears at the bridgehead with a galloper, and rides off down the canal bank in the direction of Frise. The next day he is, as usual, moving about under shell-fire when he is badly, and as it proves mortally, hit.[6] Once more the Bosch are attacking on the slopes to the NE; our firing seems to slacken, and shrapnel and machine-gun bullets begin to fall near us again.

It is now growing dusk, and a reinforcement of Rifle Brigade and Sherwood Foresters arrive to prolong our line of defence on the left – to the west – along the canal bank. Our 'B' Company, with the remnants of 'C' and 'D' Companies, is on the right or eastern side of the bridge; 'A' Company holds the bridge itself, and also the bank for 200 yards to the west, from which point the 16th RBs and 17th Sherwoods 'carry on', as already noted. The canal bridge is of steel and is lifted in drawbridge fashion by means of two cables swung from four turrets. Beyond the canal lie a couple of wooden bridges, side by side, spanning the river and giving access to a mill, which with a few sheds adjoining might give shelter to a determined enemy. A good road leads due north across 300 or 400 yards of swamp, before the ground begins to rise to the range of hills in front of us. Half left but hidden by the wooded swamp lies the village of Hem. Yes, our position is a strong one – strong enough to please a Portugee[7] – but we feel a bit isolated, and do not understand what may be required of us.

Not long after dusk the CO, Major Fairlie, sends for me and explains

[6] During the First World War a total of 48 officers of the rank of Brigadier-General and above were killed (*Officers Died in the Great War*, HMSO 1919).
[7] Perhaps a reference to the 'retreat' of the 2nd Portuguese Division on 21st March.

that steps are being taken for the blowing up of the bridge on the near approach of the Bosch. An officer will be placed in charge of the bridge for that purpose, and I am to take the first two hours' spell of this duty. He explains that the bridge is only to be blown up if and when the Bosch are actually approaching, and I am to decide that point. An officer patrol of six men under Bunce (also of 'A' Company) will assist in the matter. Of this patrol two men with the officer are stationed 300 yards up the road beyond the canal, two more are 200 yards up the road and act as a connecting link with the other pair who are 100 yards from the bridge. It is the duty of the foremost trio to challenge and establish the identity of any Bosch approaching. They will then bolt towards the bridge shouting, 'London, London'. This cry will be taken up in turn by the other pairs, and thus come to my ears. I have to get all our people across, if possible! But in any event the bridge must not fall into the hands of the Bosch. So much for my orders, which I repeat, and receive with a thoughtful salute. The six men for the patrol are soon picked and include my Sergeant Randle, and also Cpl Durrafield of (my) No. 3 Platoon, now doing duty with No. 1 Platoon.

I have a look around the bridges and get into touch with an RE officer who has the electrical contact wires already in position, and is waiting for me to give the word for the demolition. In consultation with him a barricade is erected on the principal bridge across the river, and a partial block is to be placed on the side bridge, leaving room if necessary for a stretcher case to pass by and over the bridges. I summon ten men to this work of barricade building, on which all are soon busily engaged. The barricade on the main bridge is made from baulks of timber lying near by and we are preparing rope lashings to make it secure. The blocking of the side bridge is going on steadily with similar material. Suddenly we hear a shout from up the road! A shot or two are fired! All our working party are on the wrong side of the barricade, and there is a bit of a stampede as we hear the patrol party racing down the road with shouts of 'London!' I charge across the side bridge and revolver in hand take up a position on the main river bridge under shelter of the barricade, ready to cover the retreat of the patrol party should the last men be hard pressed. I recognise Sgt Randle and shout, 'Is Bunce clear?' 'Yes,' replies Bunce himself. 'Are you quite sure it is the Bosches?' 'Yes, we saw them and got no answer to our challenge. So we fired!' By this time I am leaving the river bridge. One last question, 'Is the patrol party all clear?' 'Yes.' I am now doubling across the canal bridge. Racing to the little house where the RE officer is lodged I shout, 'London. Clear!' A second – then a light explosion, and the turrets and gear of the bridge are seen to be torn and twisted, and the two spans of the drawbridge are left pointing idly, and unmathematically towards the sky. A pause, and the TUT – TUT-a-tut-tut of a Bosch machine gun shows us that the patrol has not misjudged its target.

By this time we have all made our way back to our posts on the canal bank. To the machine gun we reply with a sharp burst or rapid rifle fire. Then a long pause of expectancy. Half an hour goes by. Next move comes from the wild duck in the swamp which give us good warning of some enemy approach. A hammering sound is heard near one of the streams, and we reply with another burst of rapid fire. Then silence, and we are troubled no further to-night.

The Battalion Diary records for this day: 'At 2 o'clock in the morning a strong enemy patrol approached the bridge which was then demolished after one patrol had fallen back. During the day [24th] the Germans could be distinctly seen moving along the north bank of the river in great force toward Curll and we punished him heavily with rifle and machine gun fire.'

[*Monday, 25th March*]

The fifth day. We are still by the canal side, and 'stand to' well before daylight with the expectancy of an attempt upon our bridgehead. With the sun-rise comes a thick mist upon the canal and river, and we can see no further than the opposite bank of the canal. Meanwhile we have had time to improve our defences, and any attempt upon the bridges would be met with a hot cross-fire of nearly a dozen Lewis guns, not to mention rifle fire. On the other hand we are anxious about our right flank, should the Bosches cross the canal at Cléry. But we realise that we can only undertake the job set before us and leave the rest to the Higher Command. None the less we study the way of possible withdrawal should such an order reach us, and decide that it would be best to make for the high ground behind us in the direction of Herbecourt, rather than risk the canal path towards Frise, with the chance of getting penned in against the canal. We have had no food up since the previous morning, but the canal water proves to be good tasting and seemingly wholesome. As the day wears on we find that the Bosch are in front of us and the noise of battle grows fainter as our lines north of the canal are withdrawn more and more to the west. In the afternoon we realise that the Bosch are moving up many fresh troops who file for hours along the communication trenches which run along the ridge facing us and parallel to the canal. At one point there is a break in the trench; men have to climb out on top for a few yards, and drop down once more into the trench. Some of our men soon 'spot' so tempting a target, and begin to test the range. At 800 yards results can be seen, with the spurt of the bullet against the white chalk bank behind. It is long-range shooting, but the chance of worrying the wily Bosch is not to be missed. And our snipers' fire begins to tell. Probably several Bosch are hit and

Riflemen in reserve.

the bodies lie hidden from us by a fold of the ground. The Bosch climb
up gaily enough. When they are faced with the results of our sniping
not a few turn quickly and in a panic jump down again into the trench
whence they came. So the game goes on for hours! At length one man
appears more leisurely than the others. As he steps across he suddenly
drops. 'He's hit! He's hit!' say several. Not so! He has merely stooped
to spread out on the ground a newspaper, to which he points derisively
as he drops into the sheltering trench! Yes, his was a cool hand, but it
needs a bit of luck as well as good shooting to hit a man at 800 yards.

As the evening draws on we receive orders to be prepared to move
at a moment's notice. Fortunately, rations in the form of bully beef and
biscuit arrive, and are very welcome.

Meanwhile, we further improve our means of defence near the bridge,
and the job is given to me of setting up a Lewis gun team's shelter on
the bridge itself. This is easy enough, for a number of solid, square
stone setts are lying near at hand, and a good breastwork is soon built,
inconspicuous and bullet-proof.

Late in the evening comes the order to withdraw our posts. Before
this is done we fire a stray shot or two at intervals for half an hour, just
to leave the impression that we are still on the spot, and alert. There is
a moon to-night, waxing towards the full. But at the critical time it is

partly shaded by light clouds. We assemble by the roadside in the little village, and march off to the high ground to the south, with 'A' Company leading. About a mile or so we travel, off the highroad, across open downland. Then we drop into a deep and old French communication trench, running due east and west, and thus lying parallel with the canal. Apparently we are once more forming a defensive flank, in view of the long distance by which the Bosch on the northern side of the river overlap our flank. We find good dugout accommodation in the trench, and all get some hours of rest. Our instructions seem to show that we are liable to attack on either side of our trench.

With the rations this evening there arrive two letters. One is from Maud, and one from Clara. The links with home seem very strained after what we have gone through, and in view of what we expect on the morrow. By this time the troops are rested, and even in merry mood. One had a football, a relic of Peronne, tied to the sling of his rifle. What a fearsome bomb it must look in the eyes of a short-sighted Hun!

[*Tuesday, 26th March*]

Surprise and a rout. We rise in good time and make a breakfast of chunks of 'bully' and bread, and then begin to wonder what we are to defend ourselves against, and whence the attack will come. We get up some spare ammunition and are just serving it out when suddenly the word comes that the Bosch are coming in force down both sides of the trench, and that we must 'get out sharp' unless we are to be trapped. Ours is an old French communication trench, so deep that one cannot see out of it. It is zig-zagged slightly, but the general direction is straight E. and W. and it offers no prospect of defence against an all-round attack. As Second in Command of the Company it is my job to bring up the rear, and with Sgt Williams, acting Sgt Major, I see that all the men have been roused and are clear of the trench down which we move. Our programme is a bit hazy, for our orders have come suddenly, and no senior officers are to be seen. Moving on down the trench, at length we get out on top under machine-gun fire and turn our steps towards a trench which seems to present a front to the oncoming Bosches. But Fritz is coming on a bit too fast, and must be checked. I find Barber of 'B' Company beginning this good work with a section of men. Collecting eight or ten of our men, I join in the fun, and Barber and I agree hastily to retire by alternate sections, each giving the other covering fire in turn. (The Bosch has apparently crossed the canal in force at Brie and other points and is driving due west down the direct road to Amiens. His immediate object is to pin us against the canal, in the direction of Cappy, and thus prevent all chance of escape, or even of useful defence. His men are pouring in extended order out of the village of Herbecourt.)

My men are firing at 400 yards, both sides standing or kneeling in the open, and several men on our side are 'winged', mainly by machine-gun bullets. My glasses show me that our bullets are falling short. I say to Cpl Laurie and the others, 'Put up your sights to 500 yards'. Cpl Laurie fires again, and a Bosch dropping his rifle goes hopping off with a bullet in the leg! A minute after I say, 'Well done, Laurie! Give them another!' Ruefully he points to his right arm, and I see that he has got a bullet through the elbow! So I am afraid the Bosches are quits, with him at any rate.

We reach our trench, and the Bosch are checked and get into some dead ground about 600 yards away. Meanwhile we are able to sort ourselves up a little and to hold a conference. Leppan, my OC Company, is of the opinion that with a defensive flank already overlapped by the enemy, we must fall back, gradually and in the best order we can. Above all we must keep clear of Cappy, and must edge away towards Dompierre. With that end in view he drops back some 600 yards, and leaves me with a strong section to keep touch with the Herts on our right and to hold up the Bosches until he has taken post. The Sherwoods on our left have already retired, as machine-gun fire was being directed upon them from front and rear! We are well placed and worry the Bosch who are still streaming out of the village at 1,000 yards distance. A message reaches me from a Cambs officer to 'hold on until nightfall'. But as I already have my orders, and have no left flank of any kind, I begin to withdraw when my own Company has reached its rear position. But the situation has become very confused at the point to which we withdraw; the troops on our left have all come in on top of us. Next we find other troops on our right coming back fast, with the Bosch driving in hard to force them to the north against the canal. It must be owned that as the troops get more and more mixed, order is fast disappearing. There is now a steady stream of stragglers flitting to the rear. One Scottish officer, revolver in hand, rallies the men. But the Bosch can be seen coming round fast on both flanks, he has machine guns already in position, and the men are mixed up in bewildered groups. Retirement is degenerating into a rout, and reluctantly we own that we must follow the fugitive stream, until we can reach a spot on which to re-form and re-group our men. It is a humiliating and exasperating half-hour! Not a Senior officer is to be seen anywhere, and we can but guess at our line of withdrawal and at what we are expected to so. Apparently our rout, for such it is, is expected by the Authorities, for the Bosch have come in on our flanks and rear, and crumpled us up without a chance of holding them. Our stream of fugitives finds a Gloucester Battalion and machine gunners drawn up in a line of trenches to fight a rearguard action, and cover the retreat. On their lines we sort out our KRRs and re-form. But our offer to join in the defence is declined, and we are told to withdraw further to 'dead' ground and await orders. On we move, now in military formation. (Though our men have literally been driven from the field where they had found themselves with no definite formation or orders, they have come away without dishonour. Each man has his rifle and his pouches full of ammunition; he is not dismayed and is perfectly ready to put up a fight when and where he has a sporting chance. All the Lewis guns and most of the panniers of ammunition have been duly brought out of the scramble, for such it was. It is a sorry show while it lasts, and there is a point where in vexation of spirit I declare that nothing will make me retire further. I would sooner be shot! But the position is an impossible one from the military point of view – we were placed in the night facing north to prevent the Bosch from coming across the canal from that direction. In the morning we find him coming in on us from our flank – the east – and also from the south – behind us. We do the best thing under the circumstances – extricate ourselves in the only direction left open. Admittedly our withdrawal is not done in the best way, but that is due mainly to the fact that we are a number of small units acting independently on no settled plan, and with no senior officer present to formulate that plan.) We pass through the valleys near Chuignes and Chuignelles, where we halt awhile for a spell of lunch. Here we receive orders to fall back upon a line Proyart – Framerville, lying across the main Amiens road. We form up on this line under the eye of Brigadier Gen Armytage and find ourselves occupying well-sited trenches, with artillery to back us, British aeroplanes busily 'spotting' the Bosch positions, and a definite task before us, which we feel ready and able to do. The contrast from the morning is astounding! Our men ask for nothing better than the chance of meeting the advancing Bosch on so well chosen a site. The right flank across the south side of the main road is shaky, we learn, but steps are taken to strengthen it. Our left flank we are told is secure, and we are content. We settle down for the night, first deepening our shallow trenches. I have charge of a post with 35 men, and the over-sight of two or three adjacent posts. The enemy registers a zero line with 5.9s on our positions, and we are thereby led to dig even deeper, for he has got the range to a nicety! Night comes on, and we are burning to redeem our ignominious hustling of the previous morning. Will the morrow give us our chance?

During the night, Scott is off duty and dozing, when he receives a whispered alarm of 'Stand to' from his sentry. Kneeling up he sees four figures approaching in the darkness, and thinks of our patrol which is probably due to return. Suddenly he is all alert on hearing a hoarse whisper. 'Nicht Schut! Nicht Schut! Kamerad! Kamerad!' And four Bosch fully armed walk up with hands held high, and overjoyed at the idea of going to England! They are duly passed on to Headquarters.

Among the casualties of the day is Barber, his honour satisfied with a bullet through the buttock, and Leppan with two holes in his breeches, but momentarily disappointed at a mere graze which did not even draw blood!

[*Wednesday, 27th March*]

Retreat and counter-attack: surrounded. We wake to find a light mist, not sufficient to obscure the view, and congratulate ourselves accordingly. We like our position still better by day. Apparently the Bosch have been busy during the night, and have dug trenches about 200 yards nearer to us. Yet the situation remains all in our favour. Away half-left perhaps 3,000 to 4,000 yards off, can be seen the Bosch field kitchens, and here his men soon begin to form up in mass, apparently for an attack. They are immediately a mark for our artillery which plays upon them heavily. Overhead aeroplanes with British markings have been flying lower and lower, wheeling above us and giving far more attention to us than we can understand. Can it be that the Bosch are flying captured British planes? A little later there appear aeroplanes with Bosch markings upon which we open fire. These come again, daringly low, so that I fire my revolver at them! For some hours we wait steadily for an attack which does not come. Then there arrives astounding news. Our left flank (towards the river Somme) which had been deemed secure has been turned, the 16th Division is in full retreat, our position is imperilled, and we must fall back straight away and form a defensive flank. So unexpected is this order, that I am bound to own that it takes me unawares, and I have given little thought to any plan for withdrawal. My first thought is for the sharing up of the ammunition on our post, and then I give the order to file out of the trench. So preoccupied am I that I come away leaving my haversack, water bottle and air pillow lying at the rear of the trench where I had laid them. Rfn Lowe picks up my air pillow and brings it along to me, but it is then too late to think of going back to claim my other belongings. A haversack and water-bottle are soon replaced on a battlefield, but the contents are a different matter, and I grudge to the Bosch my only remaining luxuries. We fall back westwards from Proyart Station dropping down the slope to the spot where a forked road leads back to the village. Here we form up in a wide-stretching line, with our right resting on the main road to Amiens and our left at the fork of the road. I am on the extreme left with a mixed platoon of riflemen. A Lewis gun worked by a Scottish officer is stationed on the road itself. As I move about placing our men in positions I make a lucky find, in a small piece of ploughed field –

two sets of loaded panniers for Lewis guns. One set I send to the officer on the road, and the other to our own guns a little further up the slope to the right. They are probably relics of the previous day's retreat.

By this time the Bosch is beginning to make his presence felt, though none can yet be seen. He is firing his Very light signals from both sides of the village of Proyart, which he now occupies, and opens up accurate machine-gun fire upon us, apparently from a gun mounted in the church tower. Presently another gun comes into action immediately on our left flank and begins to make our position very unpleasant. We are out in the open except that the men have had time to dig themselves rudimentary shelters with their entrenching tools. My servant, Marden, with three others, has taken post in a small clamp-pit which seems to give good shelter from the front, but leaves the left flank exposed. Marden stands up probably with the idea of improving the position, for he is always a plodding worker. Suddenly he falls backwards without a sound; a bullet has passed cleanly through the back of his skull, leaving a gaping wound at the exit. I go over to him and find him breathing slightly, but the case seems hopeless – the wound is not bleeding. I am occupied for the moment with a movement of withdrawal on the right. Major Fairlie, Second in Command, gives me the order to get my men away, across the road, and into an old trench system to the rear. I give orders to my platoon to withdraw, whilst the men on the right give covering fire against some Bosch who show themselves in some farm buildings, perhaps 300 to 400 yards away. Directly we begin to move backwards, the machine-gun fire increases to a whistling rate, and is concentrated mainly on the road and on a small track we have to cross. Our CO, Col Le Prevost, is hit in the knee when crossing this track, and is carried off remarking that he has 'come to the end of a perfect day'! Personally I watch the bullets spurting on the track and road and cross each in turn with a rare jerk! As I have made my dash across the track I hear a bullet – probably meant for me – strike the ground behind and past me, and I have that feeling of exultation which comes with a good miss. It is necessary to walk about on top of the trenches in order to shepherd our men in the right direction. Major Fairlie is there also, engaged on the same work, and when the immediate danger is past remarks, 'That was a warm corner, Warren!' Happily few more of our men are hit. Apparently the Bosch was well round our left flank, hence the enfilading machine-gun fire, and we fall back in good order in a westerly direction for perhaps 2,000 yards. By this time we are drawing back upon a battery of field guns, which is still firing upon the advancing Bosch. The Rifle Brigade and the Herts are acting as rearguard, and we pass through into the valley and up to the top of the ridge behind the guns, and settle down there to cover their withdrawal. The teams are drawn up ready to be hitched on to the guns. Suddenly a Bosch gun is fired from behind! – and a shell pitches in the midst of a gun team, knocking out four of the horses! The position can be grasped at a glance. The Bosch is pushing hard down the north bank of the Somme and has got a field gun in position somewhere near Chipilly, firing back at the rear slopes of the hill SE of Mircourt on which our guns are placed. Instantly our gun teams are galloped hell for leather down the hillside towards Mircourt. The guns are left! And I gasp with astonishment as I say in bitterness: 'The British artillery used not to leave their guns!' But I was utterly wrong and spoke too soon. Some men remain with the guns, and I imagine they are engaged in removing the breech blocks. Not a bit of it! The teams have run the gauntlet of rapid artillery fire racing and tearing down the steep slopes to 'dead' ground in the valley below. Suddenly up the slope at full gallop comes a single team! The Bosch gun is watching them, but shoots too high or too low. It is breathless work for team and spectators – as we are for the moment. Artillerymen man-handle the gun down the slope to the team. In a few seconds away gallop the horses with the first of the guns, and the Bosch follows with a trail of shells, working his gun like mad. Saved! NO! So with the second, and on until the sixth and last more slowly leaves the slopes. We could cheer like blazes, for it is a fine bit of work, and with all his shooting not a single shell from the Bosch seems to have told – since the first. But there is another little chapter to this saving of the guns. The infantry all the time have been taking their turn. Mericourt is probably in the hands of the Bosch, for from the slope towards the river on the left come racing two or three hundred Bosch – running like a football crowd – full speed to capture the guns. In a dip of the ground they are lost from sight to us. But we can see what is hidden from them! Lying out in extended order in the brown soil of a ploughed field are fifty to sixty silent Munster Fusiliers. On come the Bosch looking for an easy spoil! They are over the ridge, running and eager. There is a swelling burst of rapid fire from the Munsters. Its effects are just out of our view. But ten minutes later twenty or thirty Bosches straggle crestfallen over the lower slopes towards the river. They have been taught a severe lesson. And not long after back come the Munsters with a grim smile on their faces.

It is our turn to advance, and down the slopes we go, all feelings of tiredness gone and forgotten. Steadily through the small woods below, which the Bosch heavy artillery is now searching vigorously. Up the steep further slope and as we emerge on the crest we come under machine-gun fire and see the Bosch advancing down the opposite slope to meet us. The range is 1,400 yards, but we give him a few bursts of fire, the results of which can be marked by the bullet spurts of dust in the dry soil. Our shooting is good enough to change his purpose and he goes to ground in some small woods and hedges and lines of trenches spread along the slope. We are but a single line, without supports or reserves at the moment. So we content ourselves with occupying the ridge and proceed to dig in there. Meanwhile we keep up an accurate fire at about 1,600 yards upon the Bosch who face us. Slowly they retire, leaving behind a few casualties, and withdraw behind the crest of the opposing ridge. One or two Bosch stroll leisurely back after the others but our fire is accurate enough to turn their stroll from a walk to a wholesome run! Meanwhile on the right our men have pushed on to a trench system which gives them a command of the main road to Amiens, and our immediate object is achieved. On the ridge opposite us the Bosch have now mounted some machine guns and give us an uncomfortable time with a steady 'swish-swish' or 'sizz-sizz' as the bullets skim the spot where we lie. Fritz seems to be getting his own back, for he has mounted a field gun and is at his favourite game of sniping with open sights at any of our men on the right who make themselves conspicuous. The Gloucester Pioneers have now come up to join us together with some RBs, and make our left flank secure towards the river, in addition to providing some supports. We have lost a few men under machine-gun fire. As night draws on both machine guns and field guns, as usual, lose their accuracy, and I am able – after several attempts – to get personal touch with our CO on the right. I am left in charge of our men facing the Bosch on the ridge with instructions to push out a listening post down towards the valley and to dig in where the men can get a good enough field of fire. This means the drawing back of some of the posts perhaps 150 yards, and my time is filled up in sorting out and re-arranging the posts, so as to get all our own Battalion together. There can be no thought of rest yet. Our men set to work with a will to dig themselves in, though the only ration to reach them is a tin of bully beef among two, and their water bottles are empty. It is getting on towards midnight when orders reach us to withdraw, post by post, and to assemble on the main Amiens road, in the hollow near a large farmhouse. My posts leave silently, and with a single runner I follow in my turn. We keep away from the main road as long as possible, for the flames of blazing stores cast their shadows freely up the straight road. We near the farmhouse, when we meet our Adjutant and Col Cooke, CO of the RBs. Our Adjutant asks whither we are going. We tell him and he says, 'Good God! where are your men? Hasn't the countermanding order reached you?' I tell him 'No' and in a quiet voice he says, 'Well, you had better know. The truth is we are surrounded, and your men must get back to their posts.' At the moment it seems quite an ordinary event of the day. Perhaps we are too tired to trouble ourselves much! I say, 'Well, I will go to find my men', and off we move to our rendezvous. There we find none of our men, and I can only conclude that they have received the word from another source.

Walking wounded.

But we find an RE dump and some boxes of SAA.[8] Here is a chance of doing a little bit. We open a box of ammunition and my runner and I load ourselves with 500 rounds (ten bandoliers) apiece. Next we move to the farmhouse to refill our water bottles. An RE Major is coming out, and fastening on to me he says, 'Who are you? What are you doing here away from the line? Why don't you get back to your duty?' I give him my name and regiment and tell him my orders, but he must needs order me 'at once' back to duty! So I reply, 'Sir, you have not the slightest ground for the insinuation that I am doing less than my duty! Here am I carrying 500 rounds of ammunition and I came here merely to get water!' With that he drew in his horns and said, 'I do not say you are not doing your duty. Perhaps you are! But what were twenty of your men doing just now in one of these barns, with their equipment off!' That was news to me and I could give no answer, except that they were sent there to get water. What probably has happened is that the men, 'fed-up' and tired, on getting the withdrawal order countermanded decide (in the absence of an officer) to get a bit of rest before going back to their posts. I have no opportunity of testing this idea, but report

[8] Small arms ammunition.

the matter immediately to Leppan (OC Company) on my return. I also take the first chance of telling the Adjutant of my experience with the Major of REs, only to learn that the RE's tale had been given first. But the Adjutant, knowing the orders he had just previously given me, thanks me for what I have done and tells me not to trouble about officious REs. On my return I go round the posts once more, to distribute ammunition and fill up the gaps caused by the absence of some of the men. Then I turn in at the bottom of the trench to snatch an hour or two's sleep before daylight. During the night a huge ammunition dump behind us has been destroyed, and the burning shells give us a wonderful display of fireworks, which we watch with mingled feelings.

[*Thursday, 28th March*]

Running the gauntlet. The morning opens fine and clear, but cloudy overhead. There is nothing we can do to improve our position, save only to deepen our trenches, and we wait for the next move to come from the enemy. Soon we have visits from our own aeroplanes, so seemingly, though surrounded, we are not forgotten. And then come the enemy machines, flying daringly low, so low that I fire my revolver at three machines in turn. On the next visit enemy airmen begin to shower bombs on our trenches, so we promise ourselves an uncomfortable time, as his short-range field gun is once more spitefully active. We have not long to consider such matters, and personally I am resting at the bottom of the trench, as much out of the cold wind as possible, when we get an unexpected order. It is to the effect that a gap of 1,000 yards is open in the enemy lines, and we are to get our men away in twos and threes as quickly as possible, SW, in the direction of Harbonnières. Immediately a thin stream of men begins to bolt from the trench, according to orders, and runs the gauntlet of machine-gun fire from two quarters, the road to the SE and the ridge to the E. Fortunately we know the country over which we advanced the previous evening, and all quickly seek the shelter of dead ground. When my men, who have waited their turn, are all just clear, I am 'cornered' by an officious officer of the Gloucester Pioneers, who tells me in accordance with orders he declares he had had from his Major, to stop to give covering fire for the withdrawal of his men. Having had my definite orders from my own Company Commander I remind him that all my men have now gone, and prepare for my quick dash to cover. I have been watching the flick of the machine-gun bullets on the dusty ground, and have noted the spot where the stream of fugitives is thickest. Then I make my bolt, keeping to the edge of the stream, and running zig-zag in case I become a personal target for snipers. The immediate zone of danger seems to be about 200 yds in depth and in passing through it I see several men slightly wounded but still able to push along more slowly than the rest. On the whole the machine-gun fire cannot have been very deadly, for we are leaving big gaps between our men as they stream out, and the machine guns are fairly distant. I have brought a rifle and 150 rounds of ammunition, and in the midst of my flight stoop to pick up a tin of bully beef, so that I may not go hungry all day. For the first time in our wanderings, I see a Lewis gun lying on the open ground, evidently thrown away: yet in justice to the man who parted with his gun, it is possible that he only gave up his charge when hit by a Bosch bullet. Once in 'dead' ground, we soon make our way into the valley we had crossed the evening before, and begin to get together our platoons again. Sgt Randle joins me and later Sgt Stephenson; the latter we had given up as being hit. We steer our way across the main road, which is now being heavily shelled by the Bosch, and get word that Lamotte-en-Santerre, on the main road, and facing us as we retire, is in enemy hands. For that reason we edge off more to the south, and follow the wooded valley in the direction of Caix. On the high ground south of the little river Luce, which we cross, we come upon men of our Division who are re-forming in fairly large numbers. We fall in with the others and the men march in fours down the road, through Ignaucourt, to Happèglene. The village of Ignaucourt is full of troops, and there is a large military hospital there still busily receiving wounded cases. 'Brass hats' are just leaving the village in gorgeous motor cars, with rubber baths and other luxuries stacked on the roof! Here too can be seen that most pitiful of all the sights of war – the civilian population fleeing for their lives. It is a pretty village untouched by war, and a number of the cottage doors open on to the winding street. Here is a table, neat and ready laid – the coffee pot, loaf and butter yet on the table ready for déjeuner. Next door perhaps there is the sewing machine with a garment or piece of work spread out on it – left unfinished. The alarm has been given and the villagers have jumped up straightaway to join the stream of refugees. One family bolder than the rest is but now setting out westwards on its journey to safety. Maman with firm if careworn face framed with silvery hair, takes command, whilst Monsieur jabbers vociferously but ineffectually. A pretty girl of 16 had a rope over her shoulder hitched on to the hand-cart bearing the few household goods and another rope is tied to the collar of a faithful dog. All is ready and Maman gives the word for the retreat to begin. The front door is left open, as is the custom all along the road we travel.

Enemy shells are plunging into the woods beside us as we wind down the hill to the valley, and we do not pause in the village itself, but make for some 'dead' ground under the shelter of the slopes of the hill. Here is our Brigadier, and some staff officers. Quickly the Battalions are sorted up, water bottles are filled at the stream and we fall in. Few have had any rest during the night, and it is but slowly we march off to take up some new position. Meanwhile the enemy artillery is searching the opposite slopes of the little valley, and there are casualties among the troops of another Division which is retiring that way.

Our Brigadier himself leads the way, northwards apparently to take up a position between Ignaucourt and Marcelcave. Finally we are posted along a sunken road, with the Cheshires swung round to the right, strongly posted against a bank, so that they can fire obliquely across our front; there is a small reserve in the wood to our left rear.

To reach this spot we have come through the most delightful little gorge, with steep chalk cliffs, from the foot of which gushes the purest of springs, cool and inviting. Here apparently is one of the sources of the little river Luce. The trees and shrubs lining the steep slopes, mossy banks, and ferns in dripping, shady nooks, all give life to the map-name of this favoured spot – Happèglene. As a contrast to the beauties of the place one has only to note the crash of high explosive on the southern side of the little valley which forks here in two directions. Our men are gaunt and weary, unwashed and with eight days' growth of beard, their lips raw and deeply chapped by reason of the salted bully beef they have gnawed, and the coldness of the March winds. Most are limping painfully, for few have a change of socks with them or have had their boots off for eight days or nights. Over and over again we have been promised a relief which never comes, until a numbness of sensation has come over all; they obey orders mechanically, but sink fast asleep when opportunity offers. Our one great blessing has been a plentiful supply of water, for the canal has proved from time to time a good, untainted source.

Now our Brigadier is leading the remnants of our force in person, and we know that something serious is in store for us. Of the 17th KRR there are 14 other ranks, in addition to officers, but we hear that another party of about 30 has taken a different direction. Of the 16th Rifle Brigade there are 22, and these are placed in reserve. We line up on top of the sunken road, glad of a spell of rest, and patiently wait events. The ridge away to the south of us, beyond the little valley and river Luce, is held by our troops, and open ground as far as the skyline on the left is covered by other troops.

Soon the advance of Bosch forces becomes more and more plain. The troops to the right of us are engaged, and here the fight sways to and fro, until at length a Bosch battery of field artillery appears on the skyline within full view of us, but out of rifle range, and begins to snipe at our right with open sights. Then at length our right is withdrawn somewhat, slightly bending back from the line on which we are settled. Next comes an advance of Bosch infantry immediately on our front. They appear at first at about 2,000 yards distance, and disregarding us advance in solid mass to 1,600 yards range whereupon we open a few bursts of fire, which seems to unsettle their plans, for the transport which is following close behind wheels about and disappears behind a wood. It is then our turn for attention from the field gun batteries which plaster the wood only 70 yards behind us with a thick hail of shrapnel and high explosive. Trees are shorn off with direct hits from shell and come crashing down, and the shells go tearing and rending their way into the heart of the wood. They are passing but a few feet above our heads, yet not a man in the sunken road is hit. Once more we get a massed target at about 1,600 yards' range, and again we open fire. The Bosch seems puzzled, and soon some aeroplanes come buzzing and wheeling over us, and even attempt to drop bombs into our snug little road. A field gun devotes itself to getting the range of our road, yet in spite of some narrow misses, both short and over, not a single shell explodes in the road. Meanwhile we know that our orders are to hang on to our present positions, and we are sending urgent messages for a supply of ammunition which is running very low. As dusk draws on we see the Bosches line up with skirmishers in front and solid masses following in column formation, as if for an attack on our left and immediate front. His strength appears to be about two Battalions, and our thinned ranks, and shortage of ammunition make the prospects seem none too rosy for us. It is now raining steadily. The Bosch skirmishers are about 600 yards away lining a hedge which runs parallel to our front. He is working his troops steadily into the shelter of a wood half left, as we face. We spend a number of rounds upon this wood before the darkness falls. Then we cease firing, and await patiently the expected attack. We have now an average of 15 rounds per man!

Swords are fixed. We lie on the forward edge of the sunken road, straining our eyes into the gloom. An hour goes by. Then I see a movement on our immediate front. Yes, I am sure of it, and give the word, 'Here they come! Rapid fire!' Previously, word has been passed to husband ammunition and warning has been given not to shoot unless a target can be seen. A fair burst of rapid fire, and for myself I fire deliberately and low, for the tendency with night shooting is always to fire high. Now there is nothing to be seen and the word is passed 'Cease firing'. We wait expectantly and nothing further happens. Almost we think we must have been deceived. But a half an hour or so later a wounded Bosch crawls in to the Gloucesters on our right. He gives himself up – with five bullet holes in him! He was, it seems, one of a patrol sent out to test our strength, and was hit when crossing our front. So our watchfulness has been rewarded, and the Bosch attack is perhaps nipped in the bud. Still we wait in the pouring rain, now chilled and soaked through for the most part. Apparently the troops to the right and left of us have been withdrawn, for Bosch Very lights are being sent up far behind us on each flank. We are too numbed and weary to let this fact worry us much. Probably our chief thought is whether any rations, ammunition, or relief will reach us, and when? At last the Rifle Brigade – 22 men – come up from support to join us, and small though the force is their arrival is quite cheering. They are able to spare us an extra 20 rounds of ammunition per man.

I have been lying up with the men for three hours and am stiff and cold, so I take the opportunity of 'standing down' for a spell, now that the immediate danger seems to be past, for the Bosch will not surely come on before dawn. I meet our Adjutant who gives me the welcome news that we are to be withdrawn so soon as rations have arrived and been distributed. He tells me to attach myself to Battalion Headquarters for the night, so as to get a spell of rest, and I am nothing loth. Our one remaining stretcher-bearer, a garrulous old character, volunteers to guide me to BHQ. Rations have just arrived, and I dole out a ration of rum to the men, who whatever the virtues or drawbacks of the dose, hail it with the keenest delight. Then off I wander with my talkative guide, making our way to a fine house in the heart of the wood behind us. Here I find Headquarters all ready to move off, and I move with them. I am still carrying the 'unconsumed portion' of a 2-gallon (petrol) can of rum, together with a rifle. Seeing this Major Fairlie, our acting CO, insists on carrying one or the other, and finally takes my rifle – a kindly and thoughtful act! We move off through the woods, down to the waterside, and following the road by the little river – which the Bosch is now shelling steadily with his thunderous 5.9s – we march on to the little village of Aubercourt. Here turning at right angles, uphill from the river, we find ourselves in a fine trench system on the top of a steep slope which commands the road and valley. This we are told is the Corps line, and the trenches though shallow and but thinly wired are well sited and offer a good chance of successful defence. Battalion Headquarters occupy a good, dry, deep dugout, in the solid chalk. And so I get five or six hours of splendid sleep and awake at dawn a different man.

[*Friday, 29th March*]

The ninth day. It is Good Friday. With typical Easter weather but surely the strangest Easter I have ever spent. I am allowed to rest most of the morning in the dugout and take a spell of duty all the afternoon in the trenches. It is almost warm in the sun, but directly the clouds come over the wind is cold. Our garrison for the trenches is a very mixed crew. We have a number of REs – men from Tunnelling, Signalling, and Ordnance Survey Companies who have had portions of the trenches allotted to them and expect us to fill in the gaps. This seems to call for some re-arrangement, so that our men shall not be scattered. To-day our numbers have been brought up to about 80 KRRC owing to the arrival of a draft of 40 men from the Reinforcement Camp, and a party of our own men about two dozen strong has rejoined us since the previous day.

Early in the day the enemy can be seen streaming through Ignaucourt, and at once time he is attacking strongly away over the ridge to the right of us, south of the little river Luce. Save for the attentions of a field gun, which snipes at us with open sights whenever any movement in our trenches is visible, we are left undisturbed for the day, and the men who have found a supply of straw in the village below get a welcome and much needed rest.

Night draws on, and we are then busy in sorting up our men and making the most of our reinforcement of 40. We have to send a party a long way for rations which fortunately come to hand, together with an extra Lewis gun. I take my turn as officer of the watch, and am disturbed by the report of a sentry who tells me that an officer passed along our front and on being challenged replied 'Officer of REs'; he seemed to be testing our wire! Unfortunately I am too late to find and examine this stranger who may well be a Bosch.

Later at night I am relieved by Scott, and turn in for a couple of hours in our chalk dugout.

[*Saturday, 30th March*]

Hangard Wood and Villers-Bretonneux. It is yet dark when we are awakened, for an order has come in that we are to move off northwards to a big wood, Bois de Hangard, where we are to take up a position as supports, with the chance of remining there all day. Hastily we move off, for dawn is already breaking and we reach our wood before the light is sufficient to show our movements. We scatter and each man begins to dig himself a shelter, for we do not know at what moment we may be heavily shelled. Scott and I share an old shell-hole, which we soon improve with the aid of Brooks (Scott's servant) and Helmore (the Officers' Cook for 'A' Company). Some slight shelling begins and one 5.9 pitches about 100 yards outside the fringe of the wood; a fragment wounds in the shoulder a man of our Company, who afterwards proves to be Shepherd. (This man I afterwards met on Southampton Quay. He is such a poor, feeble little specimen that I once told him that, if he did not improve, the Bosch when they caught him would have him stuffed as a specimen of a British soldier! Yet he bears no malice, and is charmed to greet me at Southampton.)

Scarcely have we begun to make ourselves snug, when the word comes that the Bosch are pushing in from the south across the river

Luce, and we are to move up in support of those who are forming a defensive flank against his advance. We line a low ridge just outside the wood, with three small woods stretching in front of us and obscuring the view. Here we begin to dig ourselves in among the furrows left by the plough-share. Soon the enemy field artillery begins to 'strafe' the little wood in front of us, and then lifting a little his shells drop right on the line we are holding. With the first shell a man is wounded. Sgt Randle is next hit in the right hand. Sgt Stephenson is struck on the ankle by a nose-cap from the little six-pounder gun which is our chief source of annoyance. In all, six of our little Battalion – or shall I now call it Company – are hit here, before we get the word to advance. Meanwhile a box of bully beef tins and a large tin of Army biscuits has somehow reached us. In the intervals between the shelling tins of bully beef are thrown from hand to hand along our lines, until each man is satisfied. Similarly our biscuit ration is shared out, and the men lie gnawing chunks of bully beef until the order for an advance arrives. We move forward and find that the Bosch are occupying a trench probably 1,000 yards away, and towards that we begin to work our way. We advance steadily under increasing machine-gun fire from hidden positions. 'B' Company are on the right and 'A' on the left. The fighting seems more severe on the right, and on the left our men make good progress and are working well forward to turn the enemy's flank. A few men are hit, mostly in the legs, and go back hopping and crawling as best they can. We are gradually working more and more men forward on the left, when we see our men on the right retiring over a wide front. Then our little flanking movement on the left comes to a stop and presently we get the order to withdraw, post by post. This we do, retiring steadily. Unfortunately Eastman in command of 'B' Company has had his leg smashed by a bullet. His men improvise a splint from a rifle, and manage to move him to the shelter of a haystack, but he is in great pain and it is impossible to get him away. He has to be left behind, and a lance-corporal remains with him. We have no reason to believe that the Bosch are treating wounded prisoners badly. On our retirement we reform by the side of the wood whence we had begun our advance. Here our Brigadier meets us and I hear him say to our CO, Major Fairlie, 'If your men can't hold this wood, I must send them to counter-attack through it. We shall see how they will like that! I can't think why you came off the ridge at all!' There is nothing to be said, and we form up for counter-attack, about two platoons strong. We move off round the wood and open out, to find that the Bosch have already got a machine gun into one of the three little woods facing us. One platoon fires a couple of rounds at 400 yards into the corner of this wood, and the machine gun is silenced. We move forward carefully by alternate platoons, receiving covering fire in turn. Soon we are past the three little woods and out in the open. The Bosch are strongly settled on the ridge, and his machine-gun fire pins our men down for a time. Gradually our right flank works its way forward and develops a cross fire towards his main centre of resistance. Our left flank is in the air, and I ask the leave of the CO to go across and collect some stragglers who are coming back. Away I go whistling and signalling to the men, only to find that they have their orders to re-form behind Hangard Wood. I warn their officers of our needs, and go back to our men, to learn that meanwhile the CO has been shot through the heart by a sniper. He lies buried in a corner of the wood, and keenly we feel his loss. The enemy fire is still too strong for any general movement. One of our men is crawling forward with his Lewis gun to gain a shell-hole with a more commanding position. Suddenly I hear a thud and portions of him, as it seems, spurt in all directions! He doubles up convulsively and I fear the worst. A stretcher-bearer rolls over and over to reach him, and finds that his water bottle hanging in front of him has stopped a bullet fair and square, the water spurting out as I had noticed! The man is badly winded and probably bruised, but otherwise seems to be hurt but little. Our right is still working forward. One of our aeroplanes comes sailing over us and I signal our position with a towel waved closed to the ground. The airman spots the Bosch strong point which is holding us up, and our field artillery gets to work to sprinkle shrapnel upon it. A Jock officer comes strolling across just behind us. A fine, strong fellow. A bullet strikes him – the sniper again – right through the body, and in a few minutes he is dead.

But our turn is coming. A steady fire upon the strong point, and we can notice Bosch movements towards his rear. We increase our fire at 400 yards – and he begins to bolt. Then we go forward by sections with covering fire, and quickly he moves rearwards. Steadily forward and soon there is not a Bosch to be seen on the ridge towards which we press on. Here we settle down in a long wavy line, and begin to dig ourselves in. In some spots the men are a bit crowded and I am getting hold of some of them to fill some gaps where the line is weak when . . . Suddenly I am knocked spinning with a numbing blow on the back of the head. I fall instinctively rather than by the force of the blow, and my first thought is that it is all over and I am dead. I think at once of my servant Marden who was shot through the back of the head and killed only three days earlier. Then I hear someone (Gourdie or else Scott) calling 'Warren's hit! Warren's down!' Several men come running round me, including Sgt Page of 'C' Company who asks me if I have a shell dressing. I tell him 'No' and beg him not to let a crowd assemble, or it will draw fire and someone else will be shot. By this time I find I can raise my head and tell the men, 'Oh! I'm not too bad! I can lift my head.' Sgt Page dabs a shell dressing to the back of my head and secures it in position. I sit up and unbuckle my equipment which with revolver, ammunition, pouch, glasses, compass, haversack and water bottle is no mean weight. Blundell, a man I know well, offers to come along with me as my servant, and I gladly accept his services. I find I can stand well, so wishing the men 'Cheerio', I begin my journey off the field. The MO of some neighbouring Battalion has an advanced dressing station in the rear of the Bois de Hangard. Here a big pad of cotton wool is placed over my wound and I am directed to the village of Villers-Bretonneux, with its twin-towered church as its plainest feature. This proves to be almost a small town, and I find my way to the railway station. But owing to hostile shelling the Field Ambulance has been moved back, and I set off another mile and a half for Cachy. As I leave the village several English girls are still driving motor ambulances picking up stretcher cases brought down from the firing line. Of my own Battalion I have left behind five officers, including the Adjutant (Captain Lowe) and between 60 and 70 men, of whom about 40 had joined us the previous day. The officers are Leppan and Scott of 'A' Company, and Gourdie of 'B' Company, and Cleeves of 'C' Company who joined us about the 25th from the Corps School. It has been raining steadily now for some hours, and to me a wounded man the rain is cooling and refreshing, for the thirst of the wounded is proverbial. Just outside Villers-Bretonneux we pass a battery of Artillery whose cook has some good hot soup ready, and my pockets are filled with biscuits before I push on again. A hot drink is very welcome! At Cachy I find a steady stream of wounded waiting the attentions of an overworked doctor and a few RAMO orderlies. For some time I wait whilst more serious cases are dealt with. Then the doctor looking over his shoulder tells me, if I can, to walk on to Gentelles where I shall have speedy treatment. So another mile I trudge, and then walk into a large dressing station in the little Town Hall of the place. A Roman Catholic padre greets me and gives me hot cocoa. In a corner of the dressing station sits a tall, pleasant looking man in field grey, exchanging cigarettes and talk with our wounded. There must be some special cause to make any of our men hate the Bosch individually, when fighting is over. On the whole they have a sneaking admiration for a nation of good soldiers. My wound receives further bunches of cotton wool, and once more escorted by the RC Padre I make my way to a motor ambulance. There are four stretcher cases, and I sit on a small seat in between. It is a long drive with closed doors. Apparently we pass through Amiens, and it is dark before we arrive at a spot which I am told is Namps, 17 kilometres SW of Amiens, and on the railway. Here in a big tent, cases from the ambulance cars receive attention. We get more hot tea and bread and butter. It is midnight before my wound is dressed again. I am inoculated in the arm with anti-tetanus serum, and I am labelled and ticketed ready for the ambulance train. A short journey in a motor ambulance, an hour or more's wait in tents just off the station platform and then aboard a well-fitted Red-cross train! There are six of us, all walking cases, in a compartment. It takes a long time to fill the train. At last we are on the move, for Rouen. More hot cocoa, and bread and butter, and we doze fairly comfortably as we travel on all the night through. About 7 a.m. we are outside Rouen. Here we are met by motor 'buses and are driven through the town to No. 8 General Hospital. My companions in train and 'bus have been an interesting lot, and we learn much of what had been happening up and down the battle line. Two of them are cavalry officers, Canadians, splendid men.

It is Easter Sunday morning, and the church bells have been ringing for some time. In spite of all, wounds, fatigue and dirt, we are almost a jovial party as we reach the hospital and are told off to the various hut wards. In my large hut, C2, there are about 45 cases which make a long spell of work for the Sister and two VAD[9] nurses in charge. After breakfast in a large dining hall each man receives a suit of pyjamas and is straightaway put to bed, all unwashed. Temperatures are taken, pulses felt, wounds are dressed and we are ready for an inspection by the hospital doctors. My temperature is 98 degrees and my pulse 64. At length I get permission to wash my face and hands, and I am promised a bath next day! I am in a restless mood after so much recent activity, but manage to settle down to read a book. In my ward is another officer of my Battalion, Boney, who has had a bullet through his leg from knee to ankle. He is a bed case, and for once is dull and silent. By the next day he has recovered his wonted cheeriness.

[9] Voluntary Aid Detachment.